A PATH Not Lined With Roses

by Peter, Pavel and Luba Rumachik

edited by Dr. Sam Slobodian
translated by Christopher J. Lovelace

D0064308

The inspiring story of Pastor Peter Rumachik, imprisoned over eighteen years in the Soviet Gulag for preaching the Gospel

A *Path Not Lined With Roses*

The inspiring story of Pastor Peter Rumachik, imprisoned over eighteen years in the Soviet Gulag for preaching the Gospel

©1999 Baptist International Evangelistic Ministries

First Printing, December 1999
Second Printing, April 2002
Third, Expanded Printing, January 2008

Printed by:
Nystrom Publishing Company, Inc.
9100 Cottonwood Lane N
Maple Grove, Minnesota 55369

Printed in the United States of America

cover photo: Dr. Sam Slobodian
    layout: Korry Wannebo
    editor: Dr. Sam Slobodian
    authors: Peter, Pavel, Luba Rumachik
    translator: Christopher J. Lovelace

ISBN: 0-9676759-0-1

PREFACE

Church historian Niels C. Nielson, Jr, has called it "the greatest persecution of religion since the end of the Roman Empire." It is well known that the followers of Lenin and Marx—the most notable being Joseph Stalin—launched and maintained a brutal campaign with the intent of wiping out Christianity. Though there were occasional periods of thaw, Christians were severely persecuted most of the time. Tens of thousands of churches were closed and thousands—if not millions—of Christians perished. By the beginning of World War II, there were only 300 functioning Orthodox churches left out of the 55,000 that had been operating in 1917. At this same time, the Baptists were left with only two officially functioning churches in Russia: one in Moscow and one in Novosibirsk. Of course, this does not tell the whole story since many churches went underground. World War II brought a thaw as Stalin sought to win the support of the people against the German invaders.

The 1960's ushered in a new wave of violent persecution initiated by Khrushchev. The legal code was changed to make it easier to incriminate Christians. In his book, "Turbulent Times for the Soviet Church," Kent Hill describes this period: "The attack on the church went well beyond an intensification of atheistic propaganda; it included a physically violent campaign against the church and its members. Some children were forcibly taken from their parents because a religious upbringing was allegedly causing them psychological damage…church meetings were brutally broken up… The authorities subjected believers to vicious attacks in the press…." Once again, many believers were imprisoned.

This was the setting in which the Rumachik story of triumph over persecution unfolded. Perhaps because of his leadership as vice-president of the unregistered Baptists, the Soviets singled out Pastor Rumachik for some of the harshest treatment suffered by any Christian prisoner by repeatedly re-trying, re-sentencing and re-imprisoning him. At one time, he was the only imprisoned member of the leadership council. The president escaped imprisonment by spending over 20 years in hiding. This was not the case, however, for Pastor Rumachik. After every release, he resumed a public—though illegal—ministry as pastor of an unregistered Baptist church. This made him a repeated target for the wrath of Soviet authorities. Deciding to "obey God rather than Caesar," Pastor Rumachik accepted his cruel sentences with dignity, grace, and faith. Not many survived 18 years in the Soviet prison system.

The story of how he, his family and his church survived victorious is as remarkable as it is moving. Peter's wife Luba became a part of that brave group of Christians that made up the Council of Prisoners Relatives. At great risk to themselves, this courageous group of mostly women defied the authorities and made the plight of imprisoned Christians known throughout the world. Pavel Rumachik, the son of Peter and Luba, endured his portion of persecution in the public school systems. There he was singled out because of his father's public trials and imprisonments. Today, Pavel is part of a group of national missionaries who, supported through Baptist International Evangelistic Ministries, have planted several churches in the Moscow area. Pavel even helped to found one church that meets in the same cultural center where his father was publicly tried and sentenced five times for preaching the Gospel. Meanwhile, Pastor Peter Rumachik's church recently dedicated a beautiful church building that was built with the help of Christians from around the world.

Dr. Sam Slobodian, Director
Baptist International Evangelistic Ministries

TRANSLATOR'S FOREWORD

The following is a brief account of certain events as narrated by Pastor Peter Rumachik, his wife Luba and their son Pavel. The text you have before you is adapted from their three monologues that were taped in Dyedovsk in August 1998. At the time of this writing, no transcript of the original Russian exists, though that may be a project to be considered for the future.

I have inserted chapter and paragraph breaks as an aid to the reader, though it should be understood that no such conventions appear in the monologue. Where appropriate, I have also inserted footnotes at such points as I thought that some item might need explaining to the American reader. I have attempted to keep these notes as informative and concise as possible. Again, these annotations are my convention, and should there be found in them any discrepancy or lack of clarity then the fault lies solely with me and not with the true author of this text.

While it must be readily admitted that the legal and correctional systems of the USSR differ greatly from those in the United States, I have attempted to use terms that would be familiar to the American reader. It should therefore be noted that I have consistently translated the Russian "prokuror" as "prosecutor," rather than using the more common though considerably less clear translation "procurator" that one commonly finds in stuffy, Byzantine tomes devoted to Soviet law. Where appropriate, I have also used terms such as "warden," "the hole," and "segregation." My goal in producing this translation has been to achieve a fluid, comprehensible narrative that is accessible to the American reader.

On a personal note, it has been my pleasure to know Pastor Rumachik personally and to interpret for him on numerous occasions both here in the United States and in Russia. Throughout our acquaintance, his experiences have served to strengthen my own faith, and it is my sincere prayer that this account will also serve to empower all who read it for the further realization of God's kingdom.

It is our hope that all who read this book will see it not as the testimony of how man was able to triumph over evil, but how God consistently triumphs over evil through men willing to submit fully to Him.

For the title of this work we took the liberty of choosing something from the testimony itself that we thought would be appropriate: lines from a song that, as the reader shall see, has special meaning within the account itself. May this account strengthen the faith of all who read it, so that they might be able to join with the Rumachiks in singing its fourth verse:

Now this path, it seems to me, is not so hard,
And joy has been poured into my heart and fills it.
Behold, I am approaching the blessed gates
Where there is happiness eternal and the lights of eternal days.

Christopher J. Lovelace
Baptist International Evangelistic Ministries

ACKNOWLEDGEMENTS

Of course, this book would not have been possible without the Lord's grace and ultimate love demonstrated toward those who have recounted their stories herein. It is fitting, therefore, that the supreme acknowledgement for this book goes to the Orchestrator of all good things, in Whom is no variance. May the Lord bless you as He has blessed those whose stories are told here.

We would like to thank Dr. Sam Slobodian and Baptist International Evangelistic Ministries (BIEM) for allowing us the great privilege of writing this book. It was through the ministry that the Lord allowed us to first become acquainted with Pastor Rumachik and the amazing story of God's hand on his life.

For her invaluable assistance in deciphering and evaluating some of the supporting source material found in this book, we owe a debt of gratitude also to Yekaterina Kirianova. May the Lord bless her for her assistance in enhancing the quality of this book.

This book would also have not been possible without the sacrifice and dedication of the people at Nystrom Publishing, who have consistently been a support to BIEM. Specifically, we would like to thank Gerry Nystrom and Korry Wannebo for their contribution to this work.

To the numerous churches who have demonstrated support for Pastor Rumachik, his family, and the labor of which he continues to be an active part in Moscow Oblast: thanks. Words cannot express our gratitude for your hospitality and kindness. Had you not opened your pulpits, your homes and your hearts to us, it is likely that this story would have remained locked away in the memories of those who lived through it. It was through the travel among you that the need for this book first became apparent, and we thank God that your labor of love has resulted in the book now before you.

CHAPTER ONE

I GREW UP IN A family where my mother was an evangelical Christian and my father was Orthodox. This situation was quite formative in my understanding of God. I saw how my parents believed and how they obeyed their God. I saw my mother praying to God constantly. On the other hand, I saw my father pray to God only on important holidays: Christmas, Easter, Trinity Day, etc. This caused me to understand that people could be obedient to God in differing degrees. Of course, I leaned more toward the example of my mother in this regard.

My mother was not an educated woman, though she had a very sincere faith in God and constantly prayed to Him about me and all the other children. (There were eight in our family.) My parents didn't force me into anything, and I believed in God on my own. As I began to grow up, I found that I had to make a choice—I had to answer the question that lay before me: What kind of life was I going to live?

At that time, the lord of our country was the god of atheism, the god of godlessness. This godlessness was imbedded in people from the very earliest moments of their childhood. In this regard, special care and attention was paid to those children who knew something about God.

We had a Bible in our home. I also had a friend—Victor—whose family was Orthodox, and they also had a Bible in their home. So Victor and I read the Bible together since our early childhood years. By the time we were 14, we had read the Bible completely, and we had several discussions on this subject. We understood that the teaching of Christ as laid out in the Bible was a very good teaching, a very right teaching, and it really got a hold of my heart. But the world around me, the things around me also really worked on my heart. This put me "between a rock and a hard place," so to speak: I had two possible ways to order my life further.

I had always heard my mother call out my name in her prayers, as she would pray that I as well as the other children would follow the path of Christ and become Christians. As I grew into manhood, this question began weighing more heavily upon my mind: How was I going to order my life from here on out? I came to the decision that I would certainly follow the path of Christ—just not now. I was about sixteen at this time, and I decided, "Just not now, and not even in my youth or when I'm middle aged, but I'll follow the path of Christ when I am perhaps 50 or 60." So in this way I skirted around the matter of living a Godly life. God, however, had His own plans for my life.

I had very little contact with my friend Victor at this time, since he was away studying at high school; we didn't have a high school in our area, so he had to go to the regional high school. He would only come home occasionally on Sundays to visit his parents.

Peter Rumachik with his family in 1951

When I was 18 years old, I learned that Victor had ended his life in suicide. This had happened during the New Year's festivities: there had been some drinking, and in this evening of excitement, Victor left this world. This really got my attention and made me sit up and examine my life; I felt that I needed to take same sort of action to make sure that my life didn't end up like Victor's. His death shook me up so badly that I couldn't even bring myself to attend his funeral.

Following the funeral, I got work in a factory. In order to get to work, I had to go through the forest. About three months later in March, there was snow on the ground as I was making my way through the forest on skiis one Sunday. I was pondering many things about God at that time, and it was in that very moment that the Lord revealed His presence and understanding to me. I stopped right there and got down on my knees in the snow, where for the first time I consciously prayed for the Lord to would forgive my sins, have mercy on me and cover me completely with His love. I gave my young heart into the hands of my Lord there, Whom I had decided at that moment to serve all the rest of my life.

I knew that this wouldn't be easy. At that time many of the Christian brothers—and even sisters—were not only being persecuted for the faith, but they were also being tried as criminals, sometimes making them have to serve long sentences.

I spoke with one pastor who, after having baptized a group of young people, had been sentenced to 25 years imprisonment. I also knew of similar situations: I had heard about other Christian brothers in those times who suffered tribulations, persecution, and becoming outcasts...all because they sincerely loved their God and served Him.

When I surrendered my heart to my Lord and Savior Jesus Christ, His Word—the Word of God—became very precious to me. I valued it and

endeavored to know it. I purposed to incorporate it into my actions so that I would live as the Lord teaches and not violate the will of God. When I surrendered my heart to the Lord, I knew that the path before me was a path of suffering for the Lord's name. Of course, that was a long time ago, and when we're young we somehow don't realize the real gravity of these sorts of decisions.

After that, I served in the army for four years. When I got out, I married a Christian woman. Ah, what a great joy it is when two married people believe in God, when

Peter Rumachik with army friend in uniform, 1953

their children can see that they have the same philosophy and outlook on life and the same relationship to God! The Lord gave me a help-meet with the same faith and the same kind of relationship with God that I had.

Peter and Luba Rumachik wedding picture, 1953

4

In 1955, I was ordained as a minister in the city of Dyedovsk in Moscow Oblast. There were already several Christian families in the city who often met in the evenings and sometimes on Sundays to worship in small groups. These services were primarily designed to exhort the believers as we all studied how better to grow in the faith.

There were several things that occurred in our country in those days. Stalin died, and in his place Khrushchev began to run the country. This initiated several changes in the country as well as a "thaw" in the attitude toward religion. During this period, active persecution of Christians stopped, and many of our brothers and sisters who had been imprisoned for the faith were released.[1]

God then laid it on the hearts of some of the older men in the congregation to start a new church in the city of Dyedovsk. So in 1956, my wife and I, along with several other men from the church, began actively working to start a new church. God richly blessed our labors, and many extremely thirsty souls listened to the Gospel and accepted Christ. Among those who believed there was also a number of young people.

This was the first experience we had had in planting a church. No one taught us how to do this, but God through His Holy Spirit showed us how to proceed, how to live, how to portray Christ and His salvation in our actions and words. Many

Dyedovsk Church, 1958, with founding pastor Aleksei Iskovsky (pictured here wearing a beard) who later died in prison where he was incarcerated for the faith.

[1] The "thaw" was short-lived. Not wanting to seem too much like his predecessor Stalin, Nikita Khrushchev allowed a relaxation on the controls of free speech and press from the time he took office in 1953. Khrushev's decided program of "De-Stalinization" reached its apogee in February 1956, when the premier delivered his "Secret Speech" to the Supreme Soviet in which he denounced Stalin's "cult of personality." The "thaw" ended rather suddenly with the Hungarian uprising of 1956, though the dissident movement continued.

ministers of the Gospel were raised up in the church during this time. One in particular, an extraordinary servant who became the first pastor of our church, was a man named Aleksei Fedorovich Iskovsky. He eventually died in prison, where he had been incarcerated for the name of our Lord and Savior Jesus Christ.

We met at that time in individual homes and apartments. There was one Christian brother in particular who played a crucial role in this: My father-in-law Vasily Yakovlevich Smirnov.[2] He served God by giving of his possessions: namely, he gave up half of his house to give us a place to meet. This man also suffered a great deal for the faith, and in the end the authorities confiscated his house because the Children of God used it to meet for worship services.

Now, even though I've noted that there was a certain "thaw" in the attitude toward religion, atheism remained the major driving force in our country, and about three years after the birth of this new church in Dyedovsk, in 1958 and '59, the authorities— the police and People's Deputies—began attending our services to spy on them. The persecution began then as they started forbidding us to meet. They began telling us that we had no basis or right to hold worship services in an atheist country.

The home of Vasily Smirnov, where Dyedovsk church met for many years. After the authorities confiscated the building in 1961, it was turned into a municipal library. 28 years later the building was finally returned to the Smirnov family under Perestroika.

These weren't just empty words. They soon began to fine us for obeying God rather than men. In 1961, the other men and I were fined fifteen times. At that time, this was not a great sum of money: only 100 Rubles,[3] and we simply laughed it off and didn't pay the fines, since no laws existed

---

[2] The father of Aleksei Smirnov, one of the pastors of Pushkinskaya Street Baptist Church in Dyedovsk, and former BIEM church planter Victor Smirnov.

[3] 100 Rubles: At that time, the equivalent of about $175, a month's wages.

to enforce the payment of such fines. The fines themselves were really just something the officials had dreamed up to line their own pockets.

After a while, these threats started taking on a more serious nature. They would tell us that, if we didn't stop meeting, they would send us to Siberia—that they would arrest and try us for spreading the faith in a God that the authorities didn't believe in at the time. It was simply unacceptable in their thinking that there were enough believers in our city to start a new church there, and this was something with which the authorities simply could not peaceably come to terms.

We didn't have to wait very long until five of us were tried and sentenced in 1961 to five years of exile in the wastes of Siberia. God so worked, however, that our pastor remained free, and the church continued its existence. The church remained alive and strengthened its spirit,[4] though many left the church at this time, since not all were ready to suffer. Not all were ready to follow the path of hardship: Not only to suffer, but even perhaps to lay down one's life for the Lord. Not all were prepared for this....

---

[4] "strengthened its spirit" The lack of articles in Russian lends to some ambiguity here. Another possible translation might be, "strengthened itself in the Spirit."

CHAPTER TWO

As I LAY DOWN ON the prison bunk, I turned to the Lord in prayer. I had deep faith that my God would not forsake me, my family or my wife. We had two children at that time, though we didn't have our own place to live. This meant that my wife was left on her own.

All during the trip while I was being shipped to distant Siberia, I was praying that the Lord would send me now to precisely that place where in His consideration I would be needed.[5] With this very desire, I arrived in the place where I was to serve out my exile, in the northern area of Krasnoyarskiy Krai[6] at the northernmost extremity of the Angara River. There was a workers' village called Lesnikov[7] here, where I was alone in the midst of a great mass of people that didn't know God.

I worked at the forge there, and during the first several days as I was talking to the smith (whose name was Fyodr), I found out that his mother-in-law who lived with them was a Christian. She was an old woman…I also found out from him that there was another old woman in the village who also believed in God and these two were what was known as "Evangelical

---

[5] In one account, Brother Peter related that another one of the men tried for the faith at his trial had suggested that he pray for the Lord to work it out so that they would end up in the same prison. Brother Rumachik refused, indicating that he would instead pray as he indicates here: "that the Lord would send him where He wanted him."

[6] Krai: "Region" An administrative district. Note that, in American terms, an oblast is an administrative district corresponding roughly to the size of a small state or to several counties, and a krai often corresponds to the size of several states together. Generally, the krai applies when governing a large area with a low population density.

[7] Lesnikov: The name of this village implies that the area is heavily forested.

Christians" or "Baptists." Through Fyodr, I tried to find some way of getting in touch with these older Christian women. They had some kind of fellowship between themselves, but they met very seldom for fellowship and the quality of their spiritual life was very low.

Eventually, I met them, and we began holding meetings. There were many difficulties for us to overcome in order to be able to meet, meaning that we could only meet infrequently. They told me it had been eleven years since the death of a Christian brother named Yefenasy, who had been the only one around to lead them as their pastor. From that moment, they had been praying to God that he would send them someone under whose leadership they could continue a normal spiritual life under more normal circumstances. They also added, "Brother Peter, the fact that you're here is an answer to our prayers." I agreed with them, and told them how, as I was being sent into exile, I also prayed about this. It turned out that God had answered both their prayers and mine by bringing us together.

I also came to understand that I wouldn't have gone there of my own volition, considering that I had a family and that it was nice living in Dyedovsk, in the Moscow area. So in this way the Lord had sent me here [to Siberia]. That is to say, I could see that His will was in this, and I began to listen very carefully to determine what exactly the Lord wanted me to accomplish here.

After a little while, my wife and children came to join me. (It was permitted while in exile to have your wife with you.) ...And so it was the will of God that we should be there together. We decided to direct our labor toward seeing this small group of God's children grow so that there could be a church there. We began laboring among the people around us, and God was not slow in answering our prayers and those of our Christian sisters.

Group of believers organized into church during Peter Rumachik's first exile, 1963

First of all, the Spirit strengthened these Christian sisters, of whom there were a total of nine. Even one of the local workers noticed how my presence in the area had effected the old women. "These are the same women that, although they were believers, had never bothered us before," he said, "and now they're so bold that they can prove the existence of God to anyone, even a scientifically educated person."

I replied, "Praise God for working this way in the hearts and minds of people."

People began turn to God. The first person to come to Christ was a young woman about 32 years old. Her name was also Luba.[8] She sincerely believed on the Lord. It was already so cold outside that the river was frozen solid and people were walking across it over the ice, when she came to me and said she wanted to be baptized.

I began to test her a bit, to see if she could be talked out of her resolve. I said, "Sister Luba, praise God that you believe and want to be baptized! But you know, the weather outside is pretty bad. It's already winter out there. It's so cold outside that the river is iced over."

But she answered, "No, I want to be baptized *now*, because I don't know how things are going to be for me later on."

Of course, her husband didn't believe in God, and he had told her, "If you get baptized—if you accept this faith fully—then I'll leave you."

They had just had a child together,[9] but Luba was so certain of her faith, that nothing could stop her: neither the winter, nor the cold, nor her husband. She wanted to be baptized so that she could seal her covenant with God and sincerely, wholeheartedly give herself over to Him.

It was not possible for us to baptize during the day, since this would be in plain sight of the authorities, who would not only then be forced to take stricter measures against me, but who would also have to do something about our sisters in the faith. We decided, then, to have the baptism at night.

There was a stone outcropping on the Angara River that went out some two hundred meters from the shore and afforded us a small sheltered area in one spot where we all gathered together with the older women at

---

8 Luba: Peter's wife is also named Luba, which is the diminutive of "Lyubov" or "Love."

9 That is, this woman had just recently given birth to a child and was still recuperating.

nightfall. After we had broken a hole through the ice, I went out first into the river; then Luba came out and, there in the icy water became the first of our congregation to seal her covenant with the Lord.

All of this so warmed our hearts that none of us—neither I, nor the other Christian brother with us, nor Sister Luba—got so much as a sniffle from the cold. God protected us from getting sick, and faith warmed the heart of our dear sister. To this day she is alive and serving the Lord—a fact in which I greatly rejoice.

CHAPTER THREE

IT TURNED OUT THAT THERE were other people turning to the Lord during this time; essentially, these were young people...Nikolai, Alla, and others. Our services began to have many people in attendance, and this was something the atheists couldn't help but notice.

Once the warden called me over to his house to meet with him. (This was the man to whom I was accountable as a prisoner.) My wife and I had bought a small house by this time and were using it to hold worship services.

He said to me, "It has come to my attention that you have been holding illegal gatherings in your house. Therefore, I'm going to tell you right now: if you don't cease and desist from having these meetings, then my superiors will send you [to another camp] above the Arctic Circle."

The warden was also named Peter, and I addressed him with the following words: "Peter, are you aware of the fact that I'm here by the will of God?"

"I wasn't aware of that," he replied.

I continued, "That's right. I'm here by the will of God. Now, if I've fulfilled the task He has for me here, then He'll allow them to send me above the Arctic Circle. But if I *haven't* completed my mission, and you prohibit my activities as you are talking about doing, then God Himself will have to deal with you. Have you ever thought about that before?"

"Well, of course, I've never thought about it that way...."

We were sitting in the front room as we were talking, which room was separated from the kitchen by a curtain pulled across the doorway. Suddenly, the curtain was drawn back, and the warden's wife appeared with a dish in her hand (since she had been washing dishes). She turned to her husband and said, "Peter, don't you do anything bad to this man." With that, the curtain closed, and she went on about her work.

He then turned to me and asked, "What should I do? I have to give some kind of account to the directorate in Krasnoyarsk."

"Write in your report that you had a meeting with me where you explained all this, but that no other disciplinary action will be taken."

So our meeting ended on friendly terms. After that, I noticed that the warden never interfered with the worship services being held in the village. Even though Communist Party members and atheist activists would disrupt the meetings, the warden himself never had any part in this. Whenever we would meet, we would greet each other like old friends.

Although these were tough years, I was happy. My wife and I were both happy that God had sent us to the desolate land of Siberia to spread the seeds of love and salvation to people who didn't know the Lord, and that even in the cold expanses of the taiga[10] people had the chance to hear about God and become His children.

My wife and I together in the midst of suffering and hardship were happy and full of joy because we saw the hand of God: His help, His protection. We saw this not only in our own lives, but also in the lives of others who suffered for the name of the Lord. We knew that God through His Holy Spirit willed us not only to become Christians, but that we should also suffer for Him, that "we must through much tribulation enter into the kingdom of God"[11]

---

[10] Taiga: The sub-Arctic forest that begins where the tundra ends, dominated by conifers such as spruce and fir.

[11] Acts 14:22b

CHAPTER FOUR

TIME PASSED. THE FACE OF the land changed. In the place of Khrushchev, Brezhnev began to rule the country. At the beginning of his administration several changes were implemented. He took steps to re-open and the cases of those prisoners who had been tried for the faith and release them. It was at this time that I also was released from exile, meaning that I had only had to serve four years of a five-year sentence.

The church that had been started there in the taiga now had stronger ties with other Christians in that and other regions. When we left, we knew that our labor to plant those seeds had not been in vain before God.[12]

We later learned that those seeds of love had taken root not only in those who had turned to the Lord while we were there, but that the seed remained, and people continued turning to God even after we left.

We returned to our home church in the city of Dyedovsk. At that time, there was a bit of a "thaw": Persecution was ended, and the authorities stopped sitting in on our meetings.

But things continued like this only for a very short while. Once Brezhnev was comfortably installed and had solidified his power base, he began to persecute the Christians under the same atheist ideology as before. The oppression and persecutions started again. At this time, the statute was intensified under which believers had previously been fined, and a second

---

[12] I Corinthians 15:58 – "Therefore, my beloved brethren, be ye stedfast, unmovable, always abounding in the work of the Lord, forasmuch as ye know that your labor is *not in vain* in the Lord." [My emphasis]

clause was added which made provision for a sentence of up to three years' incarceration.

On a side note, all the other Christian brothers also returned from exile at this time. We were all released early. At this time, the church was going through hard times in the city of Dyedovsk. The worship services were being broken up under heavy persecution, and the church essentially met underground. We often had to hold worship services in the forest, but even there they found out the believers and disrupted the services. Police units would burst in to services held in private homes, forcefully take people out and throw them into the backs of trucks. Then they would take them and drop them off on some uninhabited road in the forest some 30 to 50 kilometers[13] outside the city.[14]

None of this deterred God's children, however. The Church grew. The Church remained alert. The Church lived by faith, hope, and the anticipation of meeting the Lord. Even though it wasn't the same as under Khrushchev, the Lord brought people to Him, and people repented. People were being forgiven. People were being saved. How the Church survived under these conditions is all documented in photographs and printed material.[15]

Soon after this new phase of persecution began under Brezhnev, I was arrested a second time and brought to trial. I was sentenced to three years' incarceration, but the term was cut in half as an act of amnesty.

This was not exile, however. This time, I was in prisons and concentration camps along with the criminal elements of society…Even the [KGB] witnesses at the trial commented, "It would have been better for you if you had been a thief or a common criminal instead of a Baptist." At

---

[13] 30 to 50 km: roughly 18 to 30 miles that the believers would have to make their way back to the city on foot.

[14] In another account, Pastor Peter related that the believers would often make their way back to the city singing hymns in a large group. As they filled the buses and other forms of public transportation, the other passengers were their "captive audience" as they shared the Gospel with everyone they met.

[15] Some of the books that talk about the persecution of Christians in the Soviet Union are as follows: *The Gospel in Bonds* by Georgi Vins (Russian Gospel Ministries), *Faith on Trial in Russia* by Michael Bourdeaux (Harper & Row), *Russian Resurrection* by Michael Rowe (HarperCollins), *Soviet Evangelicals Since WWII* by Walter Sawatsky (Herald Press).

that time, there was an excelerated program in place to put the general masses against the believers, against the Baptists. All press, radio and film was set against the believers. Films were fabricated to portray the Baptists in a negative light.[16] Of course, these were complete lies and untruths, since the Baptists were not the kind of people that the Soviet press portrayed them out to be.

While I was serving out my second sentence, our pastor, Aleksei Fyodorovich, was arrested along with some other Christian brothers. He never returned from that imprisonment: he died there in prison, in all these sufferings, immovable as a wall and like a true soldier following after Christ.

I experienced no special hardships during the year and a half that I was in prison at this time. Of course, I want to qualify that by saying a few things about Soviet prisons: In Soviet prisons, the prisoners were completely marginalized. Not only were they denied freedom, but they were also denied normal food, a normal place to live; they were denied correspondence—which is to say that only rarely were they allowed to send or receive letters. Only rarely were they allowed visitation rights with relatives (that is, with their parents, wives and children).

Whenever I would have visitation rights with my wife, I would always ask her how her faith was holding up: "Are you keeping the faith? How are you feeling?" And she would answer, "I'm happy that you're suffering for the Lord's name, and that I also bear a part of that suffering along with the persecuted Church."

---

[16] In one such well-known film, the Baptists are portrayed as actually having crucified a young girl in a provincial village. It was also a commonly held belief that the Baptists would offer their children in human sacrifice to their God. Of course, in the West, it is often hard for Christians to accept that anyone could have seriously believed such a flagrant lie; however, the reality is that these lies *were* believed, and there are many who continue to believe them today, even after the disintegration of the Soviet state.

CHAPTER FIVE

THE MAIN THRUST OF THE atheist machine in our country was against the youth and the children. The devil understood that it was absolutely impermissible for children to go to church or youth to participate in the worship, and that this had to be prevented by employing all possible methods and using any means necessary. The atheists adopted the philosophy: "If we don't allow young people to go to church, then the Church will die off with the older generation." Of course, this was because they failed to understand that the Lord is the Founder of the Church, and that the gates of hell will never prevail against it.[17] No pressures or persecutions could stop this movement; because in it there is revealed the immense love of God toward man. In the Church of God there is salvation and life: life with abundance[18], life in God. Therefore, the Church lasted through those difficult days, when persecution was redoubled against it, when persecution grew with a great fervor. It was precisely at this time that God richly blessed His people.

There were many people who were constantly giving my wife a hard time, especially the schoolteachers and workers in these atheist organizations. Their basic beef was that they wanted our children—and the children in other Christian families—to participate in the Communist organizations: at that time, we had Communist organizations such the

---

[17] Matthew 16:18
[18] John 10:10

"Pioneers," the "Komsomol," and then, of course, the Communist Party.[19] In the schools, it was understood that *all* children were to be active participants in these organizations, but our children never joined the Pioneers or the Komsomol.

The authorities—our persecutors—came down on my wife on many occasions and said, "If you continue to rear these children in this way—that is, in a religious spirit—then we will take your children away from you. We will deny you the right to be a mother and throw you in prison just like your husband." Of course, these were not just empty threats. There were several families that really did have their children taken from them. There were many who were stripped of their parental privileges. Some were thrown in prison for bringing up their children in the teaching of the Lord.

When they arrested me this time, the witness for the prosecution came into the cell on the third day to ask my opinion regarding the rearing of my children and, indeed, how I felt about children being in church. I answered, basing my opinion of the Holy Scriptures, that as Christians it is mandatory to bring our children up in the teaching of the Lord. I recited to him from memory a verse from the Psalms: "[That w]hich we have heard and known…We will not hide them from our children, shewing to the generation to come the praise of the Lord, and His strength, and His wonderful works that He hath done."[20]

He listened to all of this carefully, handed me a pencil and paper and asked, "Could you put all that down on paper by tomorrow morning?" (This was in the evening.)

"Yes," I said, "I can put that in writing."

---

[19] Under the Soviet educational system, children were expected to participate in Communist youth organizations that would be quite similar to what we might think of as "Communist Boy or Girl Scouts." The youngest children would be expected to participate in the "Octobrists" (named for the Communist revolution led by Lenin in October 1917), after which they would graduate to the "Pioneers" (Junior high age). In what equates to senior high, the children would go on to join the "Komsomol" ("Young Communist League"), and upon graduation could then apply for membership in the Communist Party.

[20] Psalm 78:3-4.

The next day, he showed up at lunchtime and said, "This document you gave me was enough for the prosecution to justify your arrest, and now they're going to try you for that opinion."[21]

So I was to serve another term. Of course, there were other reasons for this as well: For example, we continued holding worship services even though we were forbidden from doing so. We baptized young people. We allowed children to attend our services. We fearlessly preached the Gospel. All this added up to form the basis of a criminal offense. Add to that the fact that, even though there was very little Christian literature available at that time, we spread the Gospel to those who didn't know about God. (This was also considered a crime.)

By law, it was also a crime for the church to provide any aid to those who were suffering for the name of Christ. This also added to the weight of the evidence against the Christians when they were brought to trial.

This second term wasn't as the terms I was later to serve in the prisons and camps.

Life in our country under the direction of the Communists, especially the life of the Church, was like the waves of the sea, always churning back and forth: At one point, the persecution would subside momentarily only then to redouble its fervor again. The goals of the Communist powers-that-be, however, always remained the same: To wipe out the existence of the Church.

The Communists had a vision: "We will construct a happy society without faith in God or without believers."[22] Any devout Christian who loved the Lord and his countrymen could never come to peaceable terms

---

[21] Article 122, Subsection 3 of the RSFSR Code of Criminal Procedure reads, "An agency of inquiry shall be obliged to draw up a record of any instance of detaining a person suspected of committing a crime…and shall be obliged to give notice thereof to a prosecutor within twenty-four hours. The prosecutor shall be obliged, within forty-eight hours of receiving the notification of a detention, to sanction confinement under guard or to free the person detained." Strangely enough, Article 11 of the same Code states, "No one may be subjected to arrest except by the decree of a court or with the sanction of a prosecutor. A prosecutor shall be obliged to release immediately any person illegally deprived of freedom…" This means that, contrary to what the law seems to suggest, the warrant may be obtained *ex post facto* to the actual detention even though an arrest may only be made with a warrant.

[22] It seems appropriate to note that a popular Communist slogan said that Communism would eventually create "Paradise on earth, but without God."

with this. Even though we clearly understood the danger of doing so under these circumstances, we were compelled to carry the message of salvation because this was the command given by our Lord: "Go into this world bearing the message of salvation and preaching the teaching of Christ." Ah, what a beautiful teaching that is: that only with God can a man find happiness, only with Him can he genuinely be happy!

CHAPTER SIX

THE LIFE OF THE PERSECUTED Christians was characterized by having their apartments and houses searched quite frequently. Our apartment was also searched many times: Over the course of twenty years, the apartment was searched eighteen times.

Now, what would be taken—what did they confiscate—during a search? Well, they would take anything where they found the word "God" written. They would also take all letters, addresses and pictures with other people and other believers in them.

As I've already said, there was very little Christian literature available to us at that time. We had very few Bibles and Testaments. Most of the literature that we *did* have was copied out by hand, since this spiritual sustenance had to be conveyed in some way to other people. They took these things in order to drain the life-blood from the Church and take away its source of spiritual food and support.

At this time, we had to answer an important question: "Where do we go from here?" Of course, there were a few heroes of the faith who would come to visit us from abroad.[23] These heroes of the faith would come essentially as tourists, and these "tourists" took great risks. They would try to bring in suitcases full of literature, so that this literature would usually be confiscated

---

[23] One such well-known "hero" is Brother Andrew, the founder of Open Door Ministries, whose rousing story of smuggling is recounted in the Christian classic *God's Smuggler*.

at customs. When this literature was confiscated and taken for good,[24] then they understood that they had to somehow find another way and changed their tactics: They began bringing in small quantities, maybe five or ten Testaments at a time, just to be able to bring in even a little bit of literature. And if someone really had this burning desire, God made their efforts successful. Taken as a whole, however, this support from abroad didn't do much to put a significant dent in the need.[25]

So the question was, "How can we make it so that we might have our own source of literature?" The desire arose within the brotherhood to start an independent printing operation. We found men from among our ranks who set up printing presses, and we began printing Christian literature deep underground.[26] God inclined His ear to our desires, helped us, and blessed His church. I was involved in these activities from the very beginning, and I can still remember when we printed our first Testaments. This was a time of great rejoicing for all, and we thanked God. After that we printed songbooks and hymnals, and it wasn't long before we started turning out literature of a higher quality.

Of course, this soon became known to the authorities, because there was a government body in the country that controlled all printing, [and it was obvious that the literature we were putting out didn't come from their presses].

Our press was called "The Christian." Essentially, it was run by the younger brothers and sisters in the church and was [as I have said] deep underground. Often, this meant that those who labored there had to work in sub-standard conditions: there was poor ventilation and no electricity,

---

[24] In accordance with international conventions, the items confiscated in this case were generally returned to the tourist as he exited the country. The author is making a point to say that the Soviet Union later suspended its observance of these conventions.

[25] Which is to say, it wasn't enough to meet the immense need for these materials. It is worth adding that even the massive influx of Bibles after the collapse of the Soviet Union has on the whole been effective only in the larger cities that are usually the targets of evangelistic campaigns. Reports still abound that, in the countryside where over half the population lives, there are still many villages where people have never seen a Bible.

[26] Within the context, there may be some ambiguity here: "deep underground" here means "very secretly."

БЕЗ БОГА
на свете

РАССКАЗ
(окончание)

В деревне умерла старая мельничиха. Перед смертью она завещала Мартыну шерстяной платок. Платок был неновый, но мальчику нравился его рисунок: розы и другие цветы, разбросанные по светлому полю. Мартын, брал его ссобой в лес, покрывал им камень, на который клал своё Евангелие. Выходило совсем как алтарь. У этого алтаря он читал, молился и пел священные песни. Так проводил он каждое воскресное утро. В полдень приходил к нему Яков. Яша сдал экзамен, и мальчики зажили по-прежнему. Они вместе рвали прутья для метел, потом Мартын плёл корзины, а Яша собирал ягоды или грибы и носил продавать их. Кроме того, Яшу нанял какой-то землемер на две недели носить за ним вещи вовремя его работы. Яша заработал два новеньких гульдена. Мальчики припрятали их вместе с другими сбережениями. На эти деньги они потом купили новые платья и отдали в починку Яшины сапоги.

Не было конца их радости, радовались и другие, глядя на них. Бундаш терся около Яши, обнюхивал его, словно не узнавал его в новом наряде. В новом кафтане Яша выглядел красавцем. Но если кое-как, отказывая себе во всём, юнцы могли приодеться, то с избой того же они не могли никак сделать. Изба ветшала и грозила обвалом. Мальчики вошли в лесу, когда у них обрушилась целая глыба штукатурки. Вернувшись, они с трудом могли войти в комнату. Крестьяне посоветовали им не ночевать дома, чтобы их не задавило. Они расположились на ночлег в конуре Бундаша.

Лето было дождливое и доставило Мартыну много хлопот. Ему надо было следить за тем, чтобы скот не объедался сырой травой и, вместе с тем, не давать ему голодать. Кроме того, в стаде в этом году много было овец, которые вечно разбегались в разные стороны. Хорошо ещё, что Яша умел скоро считать, а то они, наверное, не раз оставляли бы их в лесу, возвращаясь домой.

Однажды вечером крестьяне послали Яшу с каким-то поручением и Мартын должен был один собирать своё стадо. Два-три раза подряд пересчитал он своих овец. По дороге домой он думал о том, почему ему в этот день так трудно было пасти скот. Он весь измаялся, бегая за ним, и не прочёл даже двух стихов из Евангелия. В Евангелии сказано: «Сын Божий пришёл взыскать и спасти погибшее. Кого взыскать, людей?» – спрашивал себя Мартын. – Если бы кто-нибудь мог мне это объяснить!»

Всю дорогу он думал над этими словами. Вот и деревня. Женщины вышли к нему навстречу, каждая за своим скотом. В стаде не оказалось овцы мельничихи.

– Разиня этакий! – накинулась на него рассвирепевшая жен-

24

but this was all necessary so that the authorities wouldn't arrest these workers and disrupt the work of the Lord.

The publishing ministry was characterized by its own special difficulties and dangers. At that time, all printing machines had to be registered with the authorities. No one was allowed to have any type of press that was not properly registered. That is to say that the government controlled all forms of mass communication, and if anything appeared in print about God, then they would track down the person responsible for allowing his press to be used to transmit the Word of God or any other type of preaching. People were also fined and imprisoned for these sorts of activities.

Of course, there were times when God allowed our printers to be arrested, and this was a cause for great concern among God's people. With the country being run by atheist powers strong enough even to have a heavy influence on other countries, we understood that there was no foreseeable improvement in the freedom to preach the Gospel. Nevertheless, the Church prayed fervently about this and maintained a great hope that things would change; the reality of the time, however, painted a very different picture.

CHAPTER SEVEN

MANY OF OUR CHRISTIAN BROTHERS and sisters endured persecution. Throughout the entire country persecution was acted out against everyone who conducted worship services without being properly registered with the authorities, and it was impossible to register with the authorities. Everything in our country was designed to make the number of registered churches grow continually less and less.

Human rights were grossly violated in Soviet prisons, though this was especially true in the case of believers. The discipline was harsh: without cause, people would be put in the hole,[27] where the food was exceptionally poor. One day in the hole we would get bread, water, and as much salt as we wanted, while every other day, we would be given hot food—if indeed it could even be called that. This generally meant some sort of "soup" made perhaps from half a potato and water, or perhaps kasha[28] made from grain and water but without any nutritional value whatsoever…. If someone were in the cell under these conditions for fifteen days, then this would weaken him considerably. This was one of the reasons why people were often sick in prison.

---

[27] In Soviet prisons, there were several different types of cells: the kamara or "chamber" could contain any number of prisoners and also refers to a holding cell. The kartser, which is related to the Latin word from which we derive "incarceration," is an inner cell containing fewer prisoners and may sometimes refer to isolation, although when speaking of solitary confinement, prisoners usually use the designation ShIZO or izolyator.

[28] Kasha: There is no real English equivalent for this term. One rendering might be "gruel," though this has a negative connotation not found in the Russian. Another possibility is the word "porridge."

I was also put in the cell many times for no reason at all. While I was there, I had to depend on God to strengthen me both in the isolation cells and in cells that were so crowded as to make movement practically impossible. There were times when it was so crowded in the cell that it was only possible to take three paces forward and three paces back, while everybody else had to lie on the floor. Often, these cells had cement floors, and people had to lie on their sides because it was impossible to lie on one's back. If anybody ever wanted to roll over to the other side, then the prisoners had to do it all at once. Once an hour each prisoner would get his turn to stand up and take his three paces forward and three paces back.... There were also cells that were kept especially cold for punishment purposes.

There were cells that were quite packed, in which cigarette smoke hung in the air mingled with the smoke of the *chifir*[29] that the prisoners would cook. The prison didn't give tea to the prisoners—from which this strong drink was made—but by giving the guards money the prisoners were able to get whatever they wanted. Because of this, the health of the believers and everybody else suffered in these cells.

We had very little access to people through visitation. The only people who were allowed to visit us were our close relatives: our wives, parents, children, brothers and sisters. This meant that the only way imprisoned believers could find out accurate information about the church and get information out was through their relatives, sons and daughters that came to visit them. Therefore, God laid it on the hearts of His children to form a committee that could inform the rest of the Church about the condition of those brothers and sisters who were in prison for the faith: this was called the Council of Prisoners' Relatives. Eventually, the Council began publishing a bulletin every month where it recounted the sufferings, hardships and difficulties experienced by those incarcerated brethren, as well as details concerning the persecution of churches in various locations.

The atheist government understood the danger of this committee, because, while the government wanted to keep their actions against the

---

[29] Chifir: Probably derived from the root word *chai* ("tea"). This strongly-brewed tea is made by boiling the leaves together with the water, rather than steeping the tea leaves and removing them.

believers secret, God saw to it that their actions were brought to light,[30] and this Committee of Prisoners' Relatives was the instrument for bringing these things to light.

Over the course of twenty years, my wife labored on this committee, the Council of Prisoners' Relatives. In its final years, she even put her home address in the publication as the receiving address for all information relating to the persecution of the church throughout the whole country. (When these persecutions began under Stalin's rule, there was a prisoner from Siberia by the name of Nikolai Mara who died. Of course, he was just one of the many who were to follow.[31])

Of course, the information regarding the persecution was not only sent to my wife, but also to other Christian brothers and sisters who served on this committee. My wife ministered on this committee by sending telegrams and letters from churches and believers to various government bodies. Sometimes, she sent up to forty letters and telegrams a day.

The atheists especially hated this committee, and they were always coming down on the people that served on it. Some of these people served time. Lydia Mikhailovna Vins also worked actively on this committee. (This was the mother of Georgi Petrovich Vins, who was forcibly exiled to the United States of America.[32]) There were also several Christian sisters who served prison time for being on this committee. Even those who had large families were not afraid that these families might be left without mothers, however, even when the fathers were already serving time. The Lord nonetheless gave strength and inspiration to our dear brothers and sisters in this work.

Of course, it was basically the women in the church who labored on this committee, and praise the Lord that they remained firm in their service, just like Christ Himself. During His earthly ministry, many women followed after Christ and accepted the teaching of our Lord very warmly, and it is

---

[30] The style of the narrative suggests Luke 8:17 – "For nothing is secret, that shall not be made manifest; neither any thing hid, that shall not be known and come abroad."

[31] The implication here seems to be that, because these atrocities had happened before, it was necessary to make sure that they were published.

[32] Georgi Vins was stripped of his Soviet citizenship and forcibly expatriated to the United States in 1979.

good for us to remember that the first people to visit the empty tomb were those women that followed Christ.

CHAPTER EIGHT

In 1970, I was sentenced a third time, this time to three years. I was sent to the city of Tavda in the Urals, Sverdlovsk Oblast. The zone[33] there was huge, containing three thousand prisoners.

When the brethren were sentenced, the only way to get them to the camps was to send them in stages by rail in specially designed cars. Our country was, in fact, so huge that this would require them to stay in many "transit prisons" on the way. It was a sort of unwritten law that these transit prisons were always so packed that there was no place for anyone to fit or even enough air to breathe. There were not even normal living conditions. (Of course it is understood that these people were in prison, but this did not negate the understanding that they were still human beings and should be treated as such. There still exists that thing we call "human rights.")

I remember the transit prison at Sverdlovsk very well, because I had to go through that facility four times as I was being transferred to other prisons. I also remember once when the soldiers had to shove me into the cell with their feet. There were so many people and the room was so filled with smoke that I couldn't even see the faces of the other prisoners—all you could see was their feet. Even the lamp hanging from the ceiling was so obscured by the smoke that it was about as bright as the lit end of a cigarette burning in the dark of night.

---

[33] In exile, the area to which prisoners were confined was called "the zone." Generally speaking, the zone contained prisoners, military personnel and civilians, and was often based around a small village.

For several days, I tried to count how many people were in this room. Now, for purposes of comparison, forty people might normally have fit in the cell, albeit they would still have been in very close quarters. On the third day, they took a large group of people out to send them on the next leg of their journey, and this gave me a chance to count: I found that there were 157 people in the cell.

This also gave me the chance to snag a spot on one of the third tier bunks. In the three days preceding this, I had slept up against the table. Indeed, people were sleeping on the table and anywhere they could find a spot. At night, when the command was given to sleep, the first row of prisoners would sit against the wall, after which a second row would sit on their knees, followed by a third row, and so on. There was only a small sort of path left so the people could go to the toilet. Which is not to say that there was an actual "toilet" in the room, rather a sort of open pit where the prisoners could take care of bodily functions. The stench that arose from the pit was terrible, but prisoners even laid down there to sleep, since they had to go so long without sleep and spent entire days on their feet.

When I finally made it up to the third bunk, it was very hot and smoke hung in the air. I thought to myself, "Now I can finally get to sleep."

No sooner had I begun to drift off to sleep, but I felt something falling all over my face and hands. I opened my eyes and saw that I was now covered in hundreds of bedbugs, and thousand of them were crawling all over the walls and ceiling. The walls were covered in blood, since many of the prisoners had smashed these blood-sucking insects against them. I wanted to sleep so badly, however, that I eventually fell asleep anyway and didn't even notice how the insects were biting.

Before I drifted off, I asked the guy on the bunk next to me how long he had been there. "A month," he replied. I then began praying fervently that the Lord would deliver me quickly from that place. God heard my prayer, and I was only there for two weeks.

When I was in these prisons and camps—even when I was in solitary—I was always aware of the presence of God, of His miraculous and wonderful help; I always saw His miraculous saving hand. Help always came from the Lord when things were difficult for me, and this was a constant encouragement to my soul.

CHAPTER NINE

OTHER PRISONERS WOULD OFTEN ASK me, "Holy Father"—for some reason they decided to call me 'Holy Father'—"now, you say that you believe in this God that loves you, right? Well then, why are you here? That is, we know why we have to be in these conditions: we've earned it. But you, you're a holy person. Why is it that you're here?"

Of course, they didn't ask this question to give me a hard time, but because they were genuinely curious. They really wanted to know why this was so.

I answered them, "I am here to serve the Lord. No one would willingly put himself in these kinds of situations. (It wasn't possible at that time to go into these Soviet prisons to witness or preach the Gospel.[34]) So God has brought me along this path so that you might be able to hear about God while I am here in prison."

Of course, while I was in prison I used every chance wherever there was the opportunity to tell people about our Wonderful and Miraculous Savior—how that, because He loved mankind, He gave His life to bring about our salvation.

Prisoners are a hard field for sowing when it comes to planting God's truth. Very few opened their hearts and received the truth of God. All the experiences they had had in their lives had taught them: "Eat, drink and be merry, for tomorrow we die."[35] There were a few times, however, when

---

[34] The author means this in the sense that now it is possible for missions teams and evangelists to go into prisons and openly preach the Gospel, whereas under Soviet rule this was impossible.

[35] I Corinthians 15:32

the Lord made it so that there were only a few prisoners with me at a time in the cell, and they listened to my testimony very attentively. I would also sing Christian hymns. My favorite Christian hymn at this time was "God, God, Give Me The Strength to Lay My Life Down for My Neighbors," and there was another hymn [that was also a favorite], "My Path Like the Others' Is Not Lined With Flowers."[36]

I remember how once when I was singing, "I Have Sinned, Oh My Lord, Before Thee," all the other prisoners asked me to dictate the words to the song to them. As I did, they all copied the song down on paper and then each one of them fastened these sheets to the wall by his bunk. They then asked that I teach them all the melody. So we ended up having everybody in the cell with these sheets of paper singing "I Have Sinned, Oh My Lord, Before Thee."

While they were inspecting the cell, the guards never paid any mind to what was written on these sheets that the prisoners had pinned up. At the changing of shifts, the guards would simply count the prisoners to make sure they were all present. As far as they could tell, there weren't any noticable violations of the discipline that was to be enforced. Basically, God simply closed their eyes so that they went an entire week without seeing these sheets of paper. When they suddenly noticed these sheets and actually read that there was some hymn written there about God they were absolutely horrified and came down on me for having influenced the other prisoners in this way. They took away all these sheets and told us that there was to be no more singing in the cell. No sooner had they left the cell, however, but we all started singing together, "I Have Sinned, Oh My Lord, Before Thee" because by this time the prisoners already had the song memorized.

---

[36] Please see the appendix for the text of the songs referred to in this text.

CHAPTER TEN

I SERVED MY PRISON TIME basically under "Hard Discipline." In Soviet prisons, there were four categories of discipline: Standard, Intensified, Hard and Especially Hard (for dangerous criminals). Under Hard Discipline, prisoners were deprived of many things: receiving letters and food items, visitation rights, etc. "Hard Discipline" was essentially the same as "Hard Labor," and it was the policy of the Soviet prison system that all prisoners work to earn their food (even though the quality of the food was very poor) and to pay for the clothes they wore. Often, a prisoner would work an entire month and still be considered indebted to the administration.

As I was doing hard labor, I always saw the hand of God in everything. Always. I always saw God's hand in the fact that He saw to it that I was never given work that was completely unbearable. For a time, I was in charge of the warehouse; now, this wasn't just some commercial storage facility, but the storage for the prisoners. This job entailed a certain measure of responsibility, since I would be held accountable if anything ever got lost or misplaced for one reason or another. All the same, this was certainly not like many of the other, more difficult jobs that were simply impossible to continue doing day in and day out.

God also planned ahead and made it so that even from my childhood I was skilled at many professions. This helped a great deal in prison because there were always a lot of building projects. I knew a lot of construction-related professions, which really helped, since they would put me on jobs where I wasn't really bothered a lot.

Whenever I was arrested, I was always carrying a Bible,[37] but I would only get as far as the prison gates before it would be confiscated. No sooner would I pass through the gates, but I would be searched, and the Bible would be taken from me along with other items that were not allowed in prison. They would put all this down on a receipt and later return my Bible. It is true that they always gave my Bible back to me whenever I was released. While I was serving out my sentence, this meant that the Bible would be locked away in storage.

Therefore, it was a real help to me that I had loved God very much in my youth and had actively studied the Word of God so that it richly permeated my heart. This is what I lived on: the Word of God that was in my heart. The letters that I received from my wife, children and close relatives also helped me a lot. There were moments, however, when I was completely denied the right to any correspondence. I received no letters from anyone, and no one received any letters from me. On one of these occasions I went to the administration to find out what was going on and why it was that I wasn't receiving any letters. The director called me in to the main administrative building to speak with him, and there he showed me a few of my letters with several portions underlined in red. Everything in red had something to do with the name of God.

He said, "So long as your wife and relatives don't stop writing you about God, we won't let any of these letters through. Therefore, you think about this and decide for yourself: the only way for you to get any letters is to stop writing about God."

I replied, "I am a Christian, and I live by God. These people writing me are also Christians, and we understand that we cannot live without God. That's what makes us reason and write this way. We're going to continue doing these things in the future, and whether you allow these letters through or not, that's a matter for your conscience to decide."

As I left, I began praying more fervently that God would bring those designs to naught, and this is exactly how God worked it following our discussion: I began to receive letters, just as I understood that my family was getting letters from me as well.

---

[37] The construction in Russian implies that the speaker consistently had a Bible on his person, not simply that he just happened to have one at the time of his arrest.

CHAPTER ELEVEN

WHENEVER I WAS ON TRIAL, I always testified about God, about how He loved me and saved me, and how He desires to save many more besides. He had done so much that I just couldn't remain silent in speaking out for the miraculous name of our Lord. The prison authorities often approached me with the proposition: "If you deny your faith in God and put it all down for us in writing, then we will re-evaluate your case and set you free."

And I said, "I will *never* do that, because without God there is no life. The freedom that you propose without God.... That's not freedom. I cannot violate the will of God. Therefore I will, in every situation, testify as to what my Lord has done in my life."

Then they said to me, "OK, then. You can just go ahead and serve out your sentence."

There were times when the investigators[38] would confiscate the Christian literature that they found in our homes and, in order to prepare a strong case against us, they would have to read our literature. I remember how at one point the woman in charge of preparing the case was Olga Kuznetsov, the Chief Examiner of the Regional Prosecutor's Office. She was, physically speaking, a very tough woman: she had fists like those of a strong man, and other people feared her because she could always resort to using her fists if they didn't answer the questions.

---

[38] *Sledovatel*: The term used here appears at various points in the text. From its root are derived the words *issledovat* ("to research") and *sledovat* ("to follow"). The word *sledovatel* also carries a secondary meaning, then, of "someone who follows you around." It could therefore convey the intention of entrapment. While not entirely accurate, translating this word as "persecutor" might lend some understanding to the feel it has in Russian.

Once, this woman came to me and had us go off into a private office. After she had sent the guards away so that we were the only ones in the room, she said to me, "I've decided that we're not going to write anything down today. I just want to talk to you, and the first question I have is this: "What would happen to me if I were to put my faith in God?"

I rejoiced greatly upon hearing this question, and replied, "Olga Vladimirovna, you have certainly done a great deal of evil toward the saints of the Church of God, but if this were to happen in your life, God would not hold back from forgiving your sins."

Throughout the course of our interview, she revealed something else to me: "I've given notice to the directorate today that I will no longer be accepting any more religious cases in which I will be representing the State." She kept her word: from that day on, she never participated in searches or handled another case against the believers.

A long time after that, after I had been released for the last time, I tried to get in touch with her. I found out from the prosecutor's secretary that she had been promoted and was now working for the Federal Prosecutor's office.[39] I eventually got a hold of her by phone, and as we talked I asked, "Olga Vladimirovna, do you remember that time when were talking once and you asked, 'What would happen to me if I put my faith in God?'"

She responded, "Of course. My views have changed on a lot of things, but I still can't say for certain that I consider myself a Christian." Then she added, "But I am very glad that you and many others among your people have received this freedom that you now have."

It is evident, then, that God worked in the hearts of the investigators the judges; and if they don't receive that testimony that they have heard then they will give account for rejecting God's truth in that day when all must appear in judgement.

---

[39] Federal Prosecutor's office: Here, I have chosen a term that reflects the American legal system. It would be accurate to translate this as the "Republican Prosecutor's office" if it were understood that this is the Prosecutor for the Russian Republic. To avoid any confusion with American political parties, I have therefore chosen the term "Federal" to refer to all things pertaining to the government of the Russian Federated SSR, rather than the word "Republican."

CHAPTER TWELVE

WHILE I WAS SERVING OUT my sentence in the camp at Tavda, my friends were able to smuggle a Bible in to me. For a short time I was very happy as I was able to read and study and meditate on the Word of God while working in the storage facility.

This didn't last long, however. Not long after getting the Bible, I found out that Operations wanted to perform a thorough search of the storage facility; so I attempted to hide the Bible somewhere outside. I wrapped it up in a bag, took it outside, and buried it in the snow. The prison system is set up in such a way, however, that all the other prisoners spy on each other, and it turned out that there was a prisoner following me, and he later went to the place where I had hidden the Bible and took it.

At first, I was very discouraged that my Bible had been taken. I eventually found out, though, that this Bible began to do a work among the other prisoners. When I had had it in my possession, only I and a few people that I really trusted could read it. When the prisoners had the Bible, however, they had no fear of the consequences and would stand in groups reading it. After that they would hide it among themselves.

It didn't take long for the administration to find out about this, and they even spread the rumor that I had brought multiple Bibles into the camp and they had turned up in several places. Eventually they found out through their network of snitches where the prisoners had hidden the Bible, and they confiscated it.

But for a sufficient period of time this Bible had done its work among the prisoners.

When I worked in the storage facility, the accountants there were the wives of the men who served in the administrative center. A few of them were very shrewd, giving me the chance to talk to them about salvation and eternal life. Not only did these women listen to what I had to say, but incidentally, they also didn't tell their husbands what we had discussed. (If their husbands had ever found out, I could have been put in isolation for agitating for them to become believers.) They didn't tell their husbands about this, though, and I don't know what effect this may have had on their future lives.

There was one of these women by the name of Luba was miraculously saved from one of the prisoners as he was trying to escape from the camp. He didn't manage to make it out of the camp before the administration began making its morning rounds, and as things were starting up in the morning, he hid himself in the attic of one of the houses where four administrators' families lived. Luba had the day off and—it being a rainy summer day, she was washing the linens indoors. The whole time she was doing this, she went up into the attic at several points to hang the clothes out to dry, and at the end of the day went back up into the attic to see how the clothes were doing. All the while, this prisoner was hiding behind one of the pipe fixtures. He himself told me the whole story afterwards, about how she came up and hung out the clothes, and so forth.

At this point I asked him, "So, what would you have done if she had discovered you there?"

To which he replied, "She wouldn't have even managed to make a peep before I would have strangled the life right out of her."

Of course, they caught him in the end, and I talked to him about all this later to find out where he had hid, how he managed to evade capture, and all the other details.

I said to Luba afterwards, "You know, Luba, the Lord truly loves you and not only that: He also protected you during this frightening situation when you were right at death's very door. God really had mercy on you."

To which she replied, "Yes!…And I didn't even notice a thing when I was hanging up the laundry."

In prison, I always proclaimed the name of the Lord openly. I prayed to the Lord openly. Whenever there was an opportunity, I testified about how God loves man, and about how happy I was to know the Lord. Even though

I bore this suffering—and not only me, but my whole family suffered with me—we were all rejoicing in our God. This is quite truthfully the way it was.

Once when the Lord gave me the opportunity to have visitation rights with my wife—this was when I had already spent over ten years in prison—I asked her, "Luba, what would you have done if you had known beforehand that you would have to bear so many difficulties, that you would have to bring up your children without their father, that I would be in prison all the time…If you had known all that in advance, would you have joined your life to mine?"

Immediately she replied, "If I had known all this, I still would have married you anyway because these sufferings are not in vain."

Truly, "He that goeth forth and weepeth, bearing precious seed, shall doubtless come again with rejoicing, bringing his sheaves with him."[40] There were difficult times, but through this all there were souls that accepted the Lord. May He be praised for all these things!

---

[40] Psalm 126:6

CHAPTER THIRTEEN

THE DEVIL, ENEMY OF ALL mankind, put a plan in motion against me and my family which, through a course of various actions was designed to instill us with fear. In keeping with this plan, there were even times when the prison officials would say to me, "If you don't stop praying to God, then we'll keep you in prison for the rest of your life."

Between prison terms, the length of time that I was able to be at home varied; there were times when those periods might last just under a year, sometimes maybe just over a year. Then there would be a new trial ending in more time to serve, followed by yet another imprisonment, and more separation. In these overbearing circumstances, the rearing of the children lay basically on my wife's shoulders. She bore this all with patience trusting the Lord, and the Lord did not forsake our family. We were never left without a piece of bread.

Even though there were many Christian prisoners who suffered, the Church had the kind of relationship with God at the time that would not permit it to abandon those among its number who were suffering. The atheists had a dream that, if they could create all these difficulties for the ministers in the Church by putting them in prison, this would prevent those men from being the bread winners for the family, their wives would turn away from God, their children would see all these difficulties and, consequently, choose not to follow the Lord. But these men were dead wrong and deceived themselves. Rather, the Church bore all these cumbersome burdens with joy, and my wife has often testified that the family was never left without a piece of bread.

CHAPTER FOURTEEN

ALTHOUGH MANY DIFFERENT POLITICAL FIGURES rose and fell in the Soviet Union throughout the course of my life, one thing remained constant in all their administrations: the persecution of the Church never stopped.[41] Even though the faces changed, the relationship to the Church never changed.

God, however, had His own plans in all of this. In my own life, I decided that even if the Lord allowed me to spend my entire life suffering for His name in prison—even if I should die there in jail—then I wanted all of that to bring glory to Him.

I was sentenced to my fourth term in 1974, this time to a period of three years. I was again sent to the city of Tavda in the Urals, where I would serve out that term. At this time, I saw that very insidious steps were being taken against me. The administration tried to find people who would lead me into discussing political matters as they pretended to listen to the Gospel. One such person agreed to carry out this type of work with the intention of revealing the designs [of the KGB] to me: he told me that they had written down eighteen questions for him that he was to discuss with me, giving an account to the administration every month on how I related to one or another of the political affairs indicated.

---

[41] The Soviet heads of state who have governed in Peter Rumachik's lifetime are as follows: Josef Stalin, 1922–1953; Nikita Khrushchev, 1953–64; Leonid Brezhnev, 1964–82; Yuri Andropov, 1982–84; Konstantin Chernenko, 1984–85; Mikhail Gorbachev, 1985–91; Boris Yeltsin, 1991–present. This means that the only Soviet leader to have ruled before the author was born would be Vladimir I. Lenin, the founder and first Prime Minister of the Soviet Union.

Even though my family and the church experienced special difficulties [at the hand of the authorities], the Lord taught me through His Holy Spirit never to get mixed up in political matters, since the devil's servants could use this against me. Therefore, I always kept my testifying focused on God and avoided these questions by saying, "I'm not a politician, and I don't get involved in these matters."

While I was serving my fourth sentence, a high-ranking KGB officer called me in for a discussion. He started off by asking me how I felt about murderers and about what God and the Bible had to say about them. I said that the blood of murder victims rises up as a stench before the Lord. At that he agreed with me, saying, "Yes, yes, that's precisely the way it is!" He then began to tell me how the administration had put him in charge of leading the investigation into the murder of an army captain in the zone where I worked. This all happened when the taiga had caught fire during the summer, and one army captain ended up missing in action when they went to put the fire out. It turned out that a gang of prison workers had stood lookout for another prisoner as he set the captain on fire....

With that, the KGB officer asked me to help in this affair. God, however, laid it on my heart to not get involved in any of this. Of course, I understand quite well that there was nothing criminal in this: if the prisoner had indeed committed this murder, then he should be punished justly for his actions, but the Lord spoke to me through my conscience and told me that this was none of my business. I answered the officer that he had been put in charge of investigating the affair and should therefore continue the investigation, but that he should leave me to serve out my sentence—a sentence that I had not been given for any crime, but rather because I was the servant of God, a minister of the church. In short, that he should leave me to serve out my term in peace.

He continued to call me in to see him, however, and we spoke three times. The officer transferred the primary suspect to our work gang and, through the brigadier, put him to work with me on construction projects. After about a month he called me in and asked, "So tell me what do you know: did you talk to him!?"

I said, "Yes, I talked to him."

He obviously took this to mean that I had talked about the things that he asked of me: about whether or not the prisoner was really guilty of murder or not. But I continued, "Yes, we talked. Whenever anything had to be cut down, I would say, 'Let's go chop this down.' Whenever we had to go fetch something, I would say, 'Let's go grab some boards,' and so on…."

After the third interview, he wouldn't allow me to leave his office. I said to him, "May I go? I've asked you not to call me in to see you." But he wouldn't let me go; eventually he revealed his true motives as he began trying to talk me into working for Operations there among the other prisoners.

"Well, you're an honest man. You could help us find out all the channels through which contraband gets into the prison: vodka, tobacco, tea (which was forbidden at that time), drugs…."

I answered, "You have many people that work for you. Use them."

But then he said, "We would shorten your sentence. In recognition of your service, we would reduce your term."

This interested me. It interested me, not because I wanted to receive my freedom in this fashion, but God revealed to me more and more of what this officer was really getting at: I replied, "I've got a year left on my sentence. In order for me to be set free, in your opinion, I would have to work for you for about a year just to prove that I was of use to you. That means that you really don't have anything to offer me." To which I added, "May I leave your office now?"

"No," he answered.

At that, he was silent as he started thinking about something, weighing it over in his mind. Finally, he launched into what turned out to be a full-blown recruitment. He said, "If you agree to work for us, we'll give you a new name, and you will write down all of the information you gather in such a way as to make it look like they are letters home." Of course, they were especially interested in the channels by which all these things were making their way into the prison, but God revealed something else to me: this was just a "hook" to get me to work for the KGB among God's people.

So I asked him, "Let's say I agree to work for you in this fashion…My work wouldn't be just here, but wouldn't it continue after I was set free?"

"Oh yes, of course it would continue once you were set free."

To which I replied, "I have no dealings with the criminal world on the outside, so I wouldn't be of any use to you there."

He sat in silence for a few moments, thinking about something. I made it a little easier on him and voiced what he apparently had on his mind: "Tell me," I said, "would my work in this case be only among the criminal world or somewhere else?"

"Of course, you would work for us among your own," he replied. "We are interested in your press, in your conspiracy, in your connections with your 'brothers and sisters' abroad. That's what we're interested in."

Then I answered him, "Citizen Commandant, I am not Judas that I would become a traitor for thirty pieces of silver. From the very beginning, God laid it on my heart that this matter of the murder was just the tip of the iceberg. I will never agree to work for you among the Believers. This is a great sin in my eyes and in the eyes of Our Lord."

Of course, just as I refused to work for the KGB among the believers, I never had any intention of working for them among the criminal element, either. The prisoners kept close tabs on all this sort of activity, and those who were engaged in such doings were despised by the other prisoners, who would have them beaten and sometimes even killed.

I had wanted to test this officer to see if his plan really was to find out just about the murder or if he did, in fact, have other plans in mind. And as a matter of fact, he had been planning to recruit me to work for them among my own. Often throughout the course of the persecution, the KGB would try to recruit ministers and pastors, and, if these men would not commit to working for them, they would dream up some alleged crime with which to charge the Christian and imprison him. This meant that there were Christian men and women who were tried and sentenced because they decisively stood firm and would not follow the path of Judas, the path of betrayal.

CHAPTER FIFTEEN

THERE IS A WONDERFUL PASSAGE of Scripture that says, "He who troubles you troubles the apple of My eye."[42] I experienced first-hand the meaning of these words spoken by God.

Once while I was in the zone, a certain captain threatened to put me in the cell for absolutely no reason at all, adding that he intended to do so that very day. Of course, I really didn't want to be put in the cell, all the more so because I was innocent. I began to call on the Lord, praying, "Oh Lord, shield me and help me. Please keep this from happening."

The captain still hadn't put me in the cell by lunchtime, and after lunch he left the zone by motorcycle to go to the city. He was riding piggyback, with the driver in front and him on the back of the bike. Suddenly, the front wheel got caught in a groove in the track, throwing both of them forward off the motorcycle. They were travelling at high speed when this happened; the driver got away with only a concussion, but the captain was killed. When I found out, I glorified God—not because of the death of this captain, but rather because God had come to my defense.

During these times in my life that were fraught with many difficulties, I saw how God always rushed to my aid, how He sent His defense. Sometimes, this didn't always happen immediately, which gave the false impression that God was being preoccupied with something else. Whenever it became truly impossible to bear these things any more, however, God always came to my aid.

---

[42] Zach 2:8 – "For thus saith the LORD of hosts; After the glory hath he sent me unto the nations which spoiled you: for he that toucheth you toucheth the apple of his eye."

CHAPTER SIXTEEN

WHEN I WAS SENTENCED THE fifth time in 1980, I was sent from Moscow beyond Lake Baikal to Chita Oblast to serve five years. When I arrived, the prison administration threatened me: "If you do not deny your God, then you will never be set free again. This is your last sentencing." I soon discovered that these words not just empty threats and idle words, but that the devil really wanted to make me cave in my thinking.

In this particular zone, they began to put me in the hole for no reason at all. Cell, after cell, after cell…Because of the poor conditions and the food being so bad, I would often leave these cells after fifteen days and have

A very thin, emaciated Peter Rumachik greets a brother in Christ after being released from prison in 1977.

to hold myself up against the wall to keep from collapsing due to lightheadedness, sleep-deprivation, and so forth…[Many of these cells were unbearably] hot, and then there were [other] isolation cells that were kept very cold.

Many years have passed since that time, and as I look back now, I remember that I didn't see the "light at the end of the tunnel" because Soviet prisons were very degrading. Therefore, I asked the Lord, "What purpose do You wish to achieve here, Lord?"

There were no doctors in this zone. The inhuman conditions I had been in were very taxing, and I had a multitude of problems with my teeth. The dentist came to the area perhaps two times a year, so that there was always a long line of people waiting to see him. Often, the prisoners there that were more influential over the inmate population would station their man at the head of the line by the doors so that only their people would be able to get through to see the doctor. This meant that there was no hope that my teeth would ever get fixed, or that those teeth needing to be extracted would ever get pulled. There was no light at the end of the tunnel.

At this time, my wife and I had an agreement that if things took a turn for the worse, then I wouldn't write any letters. This would be a sign that something had happened to me, so that my wife would take measures. When this did happen, that's exactly what she did: she began enacting steps through the Office of the Prosecutor,[43] through the Directorate of Internal Affairs, inquiring what had happened to me and why there were no letters from me.

Of course, the devil tried to use many tactics to deter her. First of all, the commander of the division where I was assigned sent a letter to my wife that stated as follows: "Your husband has denied his faith in God. As a result, he has been released. He has gone to an undisclosed city and will never return to his family. Therefore, you should not wait for him."

Of course, my wife didn't believe this, and God revealed to her that this was a lie that could never happen with me (just as it could never be the case with any Christian who loves the Lord and trusts Him). This aroused in her a great interest in finding out what was going on with me, where I was and what I was doing. When she found out that I was being kept in such inhuman conditions, she came to the Regional Prosecutor's office in Chita—only to find out that God had already been doing a miraculous work there: many churches had already sent many letters and telegrams to the prosecutor to find out where I was and why I had seemingly disappeared. There were even letters like this that had come in from abroad. My wife knew that they were constantly putting me in solitary, so she returned and began petitioning with the aid of the Church on my behalf. The Church

---

[43] Note that the Office of the Prosecutor in the Soviet system also includes many of the functions that in the US are relegated to the Department of Justice and, in this case specifically, the Department of Corrections.

also began to pray more fervently that God would change this situation, and God was not slow in answering.

Soon Yuri Nizhnii, Senior Deputy to the Office of the Regional Prosecutor, came to see me, and it turned out that he was an upright man working among these agents of the Communist machine. He listened carefully to all that the prison administration had done and was doing to me, and based on my words he drafted a letter in the name of the regional prosecutor. He further assured me that all these violations against me would cease and that from that point on I would be treated in accordance with the prevailing legislation of the time with regards to the treatment of prisoners while incarcerated.

Two weeks later, I was sent to the Regional Penal Hospital as stipulated in the petition he had made on my behalf. He came to me there and said, "Here they will heal you and pull all your bad teeth [I had a lot of bad teeth at that time], and we'll have some dentures made for you. Moreover, you'll stay here as long as you like, or until you get tired of it here. When you want to leave, you let me know, and I'll decide where to send you from there."

I saw the hand of God in this, that God through the petitions of His saints stood up for me during this difficult time. I received aid through this man much the same as Elijah received aid from the ravens day and night by the brook as he was being hunted down by Ahab and Jezebel.[44] On the second day after I was brought to the hospital, the prosecutor came to visit me and said, "Here they're going to treat you much differently—not as they did in that other zone."

I did everything I knew how, even asking that they send me away from Chita Oblast, away from this administrative district to another city or region. He replied, "Only Moscow can do that. But I have done everything within my power. I have taken every measure at my disposal to see that you stay here in this region. Here they will act toward you as they are supposed."

"What guarantee will you give me," I asked, "that they will treat me according to the law as you say? Mr. Prosecutor, could you please put this guarantee down for me in writing."

---

[44] cf., 1 Kings 17:4–7

He said, "For you and myself, there exists the Soviet constitution. While you are here, they will treat you in accordance with the Soviet constitution."

In all truth, the conditions really did change. During the course of a year, I didn't experience any special pressures. Of course, prison is prison, and it's prison for everybody. But when there was a special order from those who persecuted us, then those sufferings increased.

CHAPTER SEVENTEEN

FROM THE VERY BEGINNING, THE prison administration told me, "You will not be set free again." They could see that I wasn't changing in the way they wanted. I was witnessing about God, I trusted God, I prayed openly, and I was not ashamed of my Lord. Once more, this brought about a drastic change in their attitude toward me.

Once they called me in to inform me that, because I had sneaked a letter to my sister out past the censor, I was hereby sentenced to 15 days in the hole. Of course, this was a false accusation: I hadn't sent any such letter and only sent out letters that went through the censors. So they put me in a horrible cell that was only 3 or 4 degrees.[45] It was already fall at this time—September—and there was already a light, white frost on the ground. The cell was on the north face of the building where it was not exposed to the sun and was very dank, for they had poured salt into the outside walls while building the prison, causing there to always be a precipitation against the walls of these exterior cells. The floor was covered in dirt; though the real concern was the cracks in the floorboards, for beneath this floor there were very many centipedes.[46]

We received no bedding in the hole. Instead, there was a wooden frame that was locked against the wall by day and opened by the guards

---

[45] 3–4 degrees Celsius: Approximately 34–36 degrees Fahrenheit, or just above freezing.

[46] In a separate account, Brother Rumachik related how another prisoner once fell asleep on the floor of a cell similar to the one described here. While that prisoner slept, a mass of centipedes came up through the floor and consumed nearly all the meaty tissue in his legs before he finally awoke from his slumber. Thus, the centipede infestation in these cells presented a mortal danger to the unwary.

at 10 o'clock at night. This was the bed provided for the prisoner to sleep at night. When they opened this frame up for me, I noticed that it was completely outfitted in metal wire so that there were three bands of metal—each about 30 centimeters[47] in width at the head, mid-section and feet. As I lie down on this frame, I could only stand it for about five minutes before I began to get the shakes. I stood up and begun to do exercises so that I could somehow get warm. I didn't lie back down on that frame. Here I was in a light worker's jacket, without any covering for my head and without shoes (for although they had given me *valenki*,[48] these were too hot to wear, so I used them to sit on—seeing as how they didn't give us a stool in the cell.) There was, however, a table where it was possible to sit, and I laid my boots across it to sit down.

As I considered the situation, I understood what was going on: when they had given me 15 days in the hole, I had said that their attempts to break me were in vain, so they added on another 15 days as a threat. I knew right away that I wouldn't be able to survive 30 days. This was an isolation cell, meaning that no one would know what was happening to me or how I was doing, and only God could come to my aid. I therefore fasted before the Lord and began fervently praying that God would deliver me. (That is to say that I conscientiously refused the wretched food we were given.) I was unable to fall asleep under these circumstances. If this had been an *exceptionally* cold cell with temperatures below freezing, I might never have awakened if I should have fallen asleep. Three to four degrees Centigrade, however, was just enough to keep you from falling asleep because you always had to do something to warm up and keep off the shakes. In an environment like that, five minutes dragged out like 24 hours—but not just a normal 24-hour period. No, this was like 24 hours of intense labor.

Because I fasted, they gave me 15 more days, and then they added on 15 more days to that, meaning that I was sentenced to a total of 60 days in the hole. I remembered as I was fasting that Christ fasted in the wilderness for forty days before He began His ministry as a missionary; and if Christ

---

[47] 30 centimeters: About 12 inches.

[48] *Valenki*: a type of felt boot (similar to a heavy felt sock) commonly worn in the northern lattitudes.

could fast for us, then I would also fast before the Lord. All the while I knew that I would not survive if God didn't come to my aid.

One day it was a little warmer, so I lie down on the floor to try to get some sleep. Nevertheless, I wasn't able to fall asleep for the cold. Then, suddenly, I felt something crawling up my body. I opened my eyes to discover that centipedes had crawled up from under the floor, and, not only were they on me, but the entire floor was completely covered with them, turning it white. And they were all crawling toward me! Terrified, I got up. I took off my coat and began brushing them off, at which point they scattered and hid back under the floor. I began to bang on the door as I called for the guard. When he came, I said, "The conditions in this cell are unsanitary. Could you please either put me in another cell or give me something to kill the centipedes in here?" He came back later with a half-liter jar of insecticide, but since this would only be enough to cover a third of the room, the centipedes remained alive.

God came to my rescue on the fifteenth day. I was in the hole exactly 15 days, and God delivered me. In the cell next to mine, there was one prisoner who was considered to be what we might call an "enforcer" among the other prisoners. In that [little microcosm], the prisoners have their own laws and their own established sense of order. Before this, I had talked to him 6 or 7 times about God. This man had a lot of influence among the other prisoners, and he had sincerely accepted Christ into his heart. He was also in isolation, but not under the same classification as mine: In his cell, he was given bedding and warm clothes so that he wouldn't freeze, but I was kept in isolation…This man was able to get a piece of paper with a pencil slipped through the peephole of my cell, and on the paper was written: "Write down what they put you in the hole for and for how long. Then give me a safe address (not your home address). I guarantee that today I will get a letter or telegram sent out so that your wife knows about it. When the prisoner comes to bring you water, slip this note into his sleeve so that the guard doesn't notice." (Although the guards kept watch on them, those who brought the water were prisoners. I had started taking water some time about the sixth day.) I understood that this was the working of God—that He had come to my aid—and I acted accordingly.

So my wife came and was successfully able to petition for an audience with the assistant director of the Administration of Internal Affairs for

52

Chita Oblast.[49] He listened to her story carefully and immediately called the prison administration to have them release me from the cell. He further indicated that no other measures were to be taken against me in this matter.

So, God came to my rescue on the fifteenth day. I don't know how much longer I could have held out under those conditions, but it probably wouldn't have been much longer than five more days. I was already light-headed by this time, and probably would have lost consciousness had this gone on much longer—though at this point I was still able at least to move about.

In the cell adjoining mine, there was a prisoner from my division. He was in prison for murder. [Through the wall], he and I were able to talk quite a bit. God also gave me the strength at this time to sing Christian hymns, and this prisoner would ask me, "If you can still sing, would you sing that song you sang yesterday." And I would sing these songs....

I gathered myself in order and was released. In the evening, I had an episode of cardiac arrest, and [the doctors] determined that I also had major problems with one of my kidneys. I was then placed in the regional hospital.

Since I hadn't slept for 15 days, my nervous system was in a very bad condition. Even when I was finally placed in normal conditions where I had warmth and a bed, I was nonetheless unable to fall asleep. I would drift off on occasion in the hospital, but it was impossible for me to really fall asleep. Moreover, my appetite had absolutely disappeared. I didn't want to eat anything at all, nor could I eat anything—especially the food that they gave us in the hospital, albeit this was an improvement from standard prison faire. The doctors brought me local bullion and a few *sukhariki*,[50] and I would drink about a half-cup a day of this bullion and eat a few of these *sukhariki*. Gradually, my appetite began to return.

God worked in such a way that my doctor was a woman who had not been there long. After I had been there a month, she said to me, "I was

---

[49] The MVD. A reasonable equivalent to the assistant director of an Oblast would, in American terminology, be the lieutenant governor of a state or reasonably large administrative region.

[50] *sukhariki*: In theory, the Russian equivalent to the crouton, though *suhariki* may be of varying shapes and sizes.

almost certain that you weren't going to survive this illness; you were definitely knocking at death's door. I thought that you were bound to have a heart attack at any moment." I could plainly see that God had sent this woman here. She had come to work in the hospital two days before I arrived because her husband was a military man and had just been transferred from Leningrad to this region beyond Lake Baikal. Because of this, his wife got a job working in the prison hospital.

While I was in the hospital, my wife tried to send me a package. The prison officials, however, said that I was not allowed to get any packages: the level of punishment that I was under prescribed that I receive only one package per year, so long as I didn't violate the conditions of my incarceration. But God worked in such a way through my wife that the warden agreed and signed the document allowing me to get this package. Here the hand of God was also very much evident. She sent me honey in this packet of goods, and this helped very much in strengthening my severely weakened body. After that, I stayed in this hospital three and a half months.

CHAPTER EIGHTEEN

WHEN I WAS RELEASED FROM the hospital, I found out from another prisoner that a new criminal case was being prepared against me. My term was drawing to a close, and the devil still hadn't managed to kill me off in these punishment cells. God had come to my rescue, and the prison authorities had to take some sort of definitive action: They found people that had very long sentences to serve and simply lied to them, saying that if these prisoners would write accusations against me under the dictation of KGB operatives, then they would re-open their cases and set them free. In this way, they found about 20 such people [who were willing to write these false affidavits].

One of the prisoners involved in this affair revealed himself to me. In a sense, it was as if he had come to confess himself before me; he said, "I have committed a horrible act against you: I signed a piece of paper saying that, when you and I were talking, you spoke very badly about the Soviet courts, about the Soviet prosecution, about Soviet laws, and so on." They had promised to set him free soon after he did this.

But they lied to him. He signed the paper, and they didn't release him. He went to the KGB operative about half a year later and said to him, "You promised me freedom: I signed your piece of paper condemning Peter Rumachik…But now I don't see the freedom you promised."

At which point the operative revealed to him, "Soon we will put Rumachik on trial, and you will be the main witness for the prosecution."

He thought that they would set him free, and that two weeks before his release he could just hide out somewhere in the taiga[51]. Now that he found out there was to be a trial against me with him on the witness stand, however, it was a different matter entirely, because many of the other prisoners had a great deal of respect for me. This meant that things could get very bad for him, and that when the other prisoners found out what he had done they would beat him up or maybe worse. At this point, he became filled with rage, and grabbing the KGB operative by the neck, nearly strangled him to death. (Had the operative not been able to push the button to sound the alarm, this prisoner probably would have quite literally strangled the life right out of him.) At this point, the lieutenant colonel under whom the operative served ran into the room and pulled this prisoner Anatoly off of him. Normally, for such actions a prisoner would have his sentence extended, but in this case they didn't even put him in the hole because they could sense that they were the ones at fault.

Then he came and confessed all this to me, saying, "I have done this wrong, and now you may kill me." With that, he fell down on his knees before me and said, "Do with me as you will!"

I said to him, "I am a Christian, and I will not do anything to you. Now as far as what you said about having done wrong: yes, you have done wrong, but it is good that you have confessed it. At the trial, you must tell all of this as it really happened."

And he replied, "Yes, I will tell it just as it was."

The next day, he told me that he had already written a notice to be sent to the regional prosecutor; and there he indicated that the statement he had given was unreliable, that he had been bought off by being promised freedom in exchange for signing this paper. He continued by saying that he was also aware of the names of other people who had agreed to issue false statements against me, and that a trial would soon be opened based on these documents. I told him not to send this letter to the prosecutor, but that he should instead write a similar letter in his own hand and give it to me. It was very important for me to have a letter like this in the event

---

[51] That is, he could hide in the forest that was still within the limits of the prison camp complex so that the other prisoners wouldn't get him after they discovered how he had earned his freedom.

that I should be tried, so that I might be able to show the methods used in putting together the accusation against me.

He wrote a second copy and gave it to me. Soon after that, I sent declarations to various divisions of the government of prosecutors' offices, and in each one I enclosed a copy of this prisoner's repentant letter. Of course, this created quite a stir, and the authorities tried to accuse me of slander by maintaining that no such trial was in the works. On the other hand, they didn't put me in the hole, either.[52]

I understood that something was going on because now they had the ability to add on sentences to terms currently being served. I found out from my wife that many of the brethren in prison were not being released; their sentences would be coming to an end when the authorities would suddenly add on another sentence, effectively making it as if they hadn't yet served any of the sentence they had just finished.

As my five-year term was coming to an end, I thought that they would probably set me free. Everything had the feel to it that they were going to release me. Six days before my release date, however, a woman—a senior investigator—came from the regional prosecutor's office. She began questioning me regarding various political matters, on one thing and another. I answered that I was a Christian and not a politician, and that I had neither the will nor the desire to discuss political affairs with anyone—that I never discuss politics with others. At that, she ordered the captain who was with us to call in several prisoners. As she brought these prisoners in one at a time, she asked each one if it was true that I had on such-and-such a date talked with him concerning such-and-such political topic.

Clearly, this was all a set-up; all of this was prepared beforehand. These prisoners had been promised freedom, that their cases would be re-opened. So they lied, dragging me through the mud and saying that I was very dissatisfied with the Soviet authorities. This went on even to the point that they claimed that I was stirring up the youth to overthrow the Soviet government with the aid of various capitalist countries like America, West

---

[52] That is to say, had Peter Rumachik's accusations against the government been groundless, he would have been punished. The fact that they did not punish him in this case substantiates his claim that a trial was indeed being prepared even though the authorities denied it.

Germany, and others. On the basis of these false testimonies, I was again placed under arrest and sent to a prison for people under investigation. At this point, a new investigation began. I was held under a political statute on the grounds that I had supposedly attempted to overthrow of the Soviet government. Or more specifically, that I had talked to the youth—since we had a great many Christian youth—and tried to get them to overturn Soviet power. But this was all a diabolical scheme designed to add on more time to my prison term.[53]

And yes, my term was extended. They added on five more years, although the statute under which I was tried allowed for a sentence of up to 12 years…This was already during Gorbachev's *perestroika*, however. *Perestroika* was already being implemented in our land, so they only added on five more years.

The trial lasted for over a month. My wife and children came, but since the children by this time had their own factory jobs to work, they couldn't stay until the very end of the trial. My wife, however, was at the trial until the end. There were also a few members from our church who came throughout the course of the trial.[54] When they read the verdict sentencing me to five years, I noticed suddenly that the air was filled with flowers flying toward me from the gallery; my wife and the other believers

---

[53] There are several statutes of Chapter 8 of the RSFSR Criminal Codex that are worth mentioning here. Article 183 states, "The compelling of a witness, victim or expert to give judicial or investigative agencies false testimony or a false opinion, committed by…the bribing of [same] to give false testimony or a false opinion, shall be punished by deprivation of freedom for a term not exceeding two years or by correctional tasks for a term not exceeding one year." For "the giving of a testimony known to be false," (Article 181) the witness would face incarceration of up to one year under normal circumstances. In this case, however, the testimony in question accuses Peter Rumachik of attempting to overthrow the Soviet Union, which falls under the Chapter One category of "Especially Dangerous Crimes," specifically in question here are the following crimes: treason (Article 64), anti-Soviet agitation and propaganda (article 70), and "Organizational Activity Directed to the Commission of Especially Dangerous Crimes Against the State and Also Participation in Anti-Soviet Organizations." (Article 72) Two of these statutes carried the death penalty. Giving false testimony that accused someone of Chapter One crimes was punishable by "deprivation of freedom for a term of two to seven years." Any official making a "report known to be false" would be subject to up to three years' incarceration or correctional tasks up to one year, though in this case, the punishment could be two to seven years.

[54] It is worth noting that the trial was held some four thousand miles from the location of Pastor Rumachik's church. This would be the equivalent of someone in the States making a Trans-Atlantic flight just to offer moral support at the trial of a Christian brother.

had brought in flowers that they had hidden under their coats, and when the verdict was read they let them fly as a sign of protest. The soldiers began to quickly gather up the flowers, but I was able to latch on to one and hide it in my pocket. They took it away from me, however, when I was searched just before being put back into prison.

CHAPTER NINETEEN

ONCE AGAIN, THE LONG DAYS in Chita Prison dragged on. While I was in the cell, I waited a long time for them to send me into the zone. The prison authorities had concocted their own ideas, though. They had a plan to put me in a psychiatric hospital,[55] but God did not allow any of this. I asked the prison administration when they planned to send me into the zone, and they answered that once they got the order from Moscow, they wouldn't keep me a moment longer.

At this time, there were several cells where it wasn't so bad for me. People already knew me there, and I knew what people were like because of what I had experienced in my life here. I witnessed to them a great deal. I sang a lot. Some of them even remembered Christian hymns and would ask me, "Sing such-and-such song." My favorite songs at this time were "My Path Like the Others' Is Not Lined with Flowers" or "God, God, Give Me The Strength to Lay My Life Down for My Neighbors,"[56] and there were many others.

In Chita Prison, there were many female guards. Once when we were in the exercise yard, one of these women came up to our area and called me by name, saying, "Yesterday they showed you on television." I had been there by this time for almost a year, so they already knew me by name. My cellmates were very interested in this affair, and they began asking, "What was the show about? How was he portrayed on television?" She didn't

---

[55] Little needs be said here regarding the dangers of the psychiatric wards whose function was not to heal the mind, but rather to destroy it.

[56] The words to these songs are given in the appendix.

answer for a long while, but then responded to their question by pointing at me and saying, "Way to go!" At that, she left.[57]

I became so accustomed to being in this cell that I began thinking that it wouldn't be bad for me to just serve out the rest of my five-year sentence in that cell. Everybody had their own sentences though, and people were periodically sent on to the labor camps. The cell-mates I had there were replaced in time with new ones, but all of them knew I was a Christian. We had many discussions, and there were many questions; but none of the prisoners made a clear decision for repentance at this time.

God had His own plan about how He was going to use me here in this prison for those people who needed the Lord's salvation. Now, all people need the Lord, but those who find themselves in difficult situations like prison or in special confinement have a greater openness to listen to the Word of God. Nonetheless, this is hard ground in which our Lord's seeds are not always well received.

We knew that there were three cells in this prison: to the right of the exit to the prison yard there was a small corridor that led onto three small cells. All the prisoners knew that terrible things went on in these cells. There were people there who worked for the prison administration, and if the administration felt it necessary to have one of the prisoners dealt with, he would be put in one of these cells. In that cell, this person who worked for the administration could do whatever he wanted to the prisoner—even to the point of killing him—and he would not be tried for it, since he had fulfilled the will of the administration.

Once the guard opened the door, called my name, and gave the order, "Bring your things!" I thought they were sending me into the zone, but to my great surprise—and my horror—they brought me into this corridor. They opened the door to one of these cells, and as I entered I saw a large

---

[57] In later discussions with Georgi Vins and family members, Brother Rumachik was able to re-construct this event: The program in question was called "Brothers in the Dollar," and opened with a money counting machine flipping through stacks of American money. Through use of still pictures and other media, the program went on to portray Peter Rumachik and Georgi Vins as racketeers who used the cause of Christ to scam money from the West. The reader may do well to keep in mind that this program would have been broadcast at the heyday of televangelism in the West, which may lend some explanation to the *zeitgeist* which led to such a fantastical fabrication.

man in the cell, almost two meters[58] in height, very broad in the shoulders. In short, this was a very powerful man about thirty-five years of age. There were also two other prisoners with him in the cell: they were more or less like trained pets who gazed wide-eyed upon me to see what was going to happen next.

I entered the cell, said "Hello," and announced to them all that I was a Christian, that I had been sentenced for being faithful to the Lord, for the fact that I believe in Jesus Christ and spread His teaching; and that they had added yet another five-year sentence onto the five years that I had just served. Then I added, "Whenever I come into a new cell, I always begin my life there with prayer. I would like to pray here." The other two prisoners looked at each other, but the other one just stood there silently. I got down on my knees and prayed out loud that God would bless my stay here, that He would help me, that He would give me strength and wisdom concerning how I should carry myself here.

When I stood up from praying, this tough prisoner began firing questions at me to provoke me into a fight. I answered a few of them, but noticed that my answers weren't putting him in exceptionally good humor, and he began to get angry and try to pick a fight with me. I prayed silently to myself and said to this man, "Friend, in as much as I can see that my answers don't seem to be to your liking, let's make a deal: You don't ask me any more questions since my answers upset you, and since we both have to be here together, we'll just spend the rest of the time not speaking to each other."

He didn't offer any answer to my suggestion, but instead continued asking questions. I climbed up on my bunk, lie down and began to think. I understood that I would need special strength to detect these temptations and traps to which I might be subjected. There I prayed to God yet again while I was lying on the bunk, and turned to the Lord in fasting for my spiritual empowerment that He might be able to do His work in the lives of these two prisoners and in the life of this man who fulfilled the wishes of the administration.

Time passed. Every day, this man asked me questions, but I remained silent. Occasionally, the other two would ask me questions, and I would

---

58 Well over six feet tall.

answer—but they asked questions only on rare occasions. I noticed also how he treated these other two prisoners: on the second day, something upset him so that he struck the wooden table so fiercely with his fist that I thought it would surely burst into splinters. He could also force them under the beds so that they would stay hidden there as long as it pleased him. They didn't have the right to get out from under the bed, because if they did he might even beat them to death. I began to pray fervently that God would do something: that He would either take me out of this place, or do that work for which purpose He had sent me to this cell in the first place. I knew that I could do nothing here unless His will was in it, but I still didn't know what exactly the Lord wanted to accomplish by having me go through this particular experience. Every day, I expected something terrible from this man—some kind of awful provocation the likes of which I had not seen in all the previous prisons and camps. In a week, however, they moved him with all his belongings out of the cell; which is to say that they either moved him to another cell or transferred him to another prison facility.

There were three of us left now in the cell. Now that everybody could now rest easy for a bit, I even exclaimed, "Praise God that this man is no longer here!" That still didn't answer the question, however: "What next?" It wasn't long before I got the answer.

That very evening, they began knocking at our cell from the floor below us. In prison, there is what we refer to as the "prison mail system"; that is, notes and letters are passed by strings and pieces of yarn from cell to cell and floor to floor. In this way, notes can be passed from any one point of the prison to any other. So then, this knocking from the floor beneath us was the sign for us to lower a thread and "pick up the mail."

When we had once lowered the thread and retrieved the letter that they subsequently tied to it, one of my cellmates—Nikolai by name—began to read. No sooner had he begun reading the letter, but he said, "Peter, this is note is for you."

I answered, "No, how can anybody even know I'm here? I've only been here for a week."

But he insisted, saying, "Nope. This is for you."

I took it and began to read. Lo, and behold, it really was for me. The note began with the following words:

Holy Father Peter,[59]

I have been looking for you for half a year now in this prison. My name is Peter ——. *I am on death row, but my case has been re-opened....* He then went on to explain the horrible crime that he had committed with his accomplices. They had murdered two pensioners, an old man and his wife. Originally, they had tried to get money from them to buy liquor. When it turned out that the old couple had no money, they set upon them and beat them severely. At this point, they suddenly realized that they had already crossed the line. So they killed them and set the couple's house on fire. The house didn't burn down, however; since it was night, the fire department was alerted to the blaze in time to extinguish it. As the firemen examined the damage, they also found several other clues: namely, the old man had his fingers and an ear cut off, and the fire department concluded that the blaze was the result of foul play. Soon they had taken these three young men and a young woman with them into custody. The other three were given long sentences, but this fourth—this Peter—was sentenced to death because the weight of the blame hung on him.

After writing the details of this horrible crime, he directed his comments back to me:

I don't believe in God. But I've been wondering: if there is a God, would He forgive me? I await your answer and ask that you respond with all possible haste.

The story of this crime affected me so strongly that for a time I didn't even know what to answer myself, let alone what I should tell this prisoner. This was truly a hideous crime, and he was asking, "Would God forgive me?" But my Jesus helped me as He put in my mind a picture of Himself on the cross at Calvary between two thieves. As one of them turned to Christ and said, "Remember me when You come into Your kingdom,"[60] the Lord forgave this malefactor. This was the answer from the Lord that I was to convey to this man.

I sat down straightaway and wrote him a letter in which I quite confidently and firmly answered that God was ready to forgive him if, in full consciousness of his actions, he would only repent before the Lord—if

---

[59] Note that this is simply a nickname. The addressee referred to is not a priest.

[60] Luke 23:42–43 "And he said unto Jesus, Lord, remember me when thou comest into thy kingdom. And Jesus said unto him, Verily I say unto thee, To day shalt thou be with me in paradise."

he would turn his face toward the Lord and know that God loves him. Even though he had committed such a horrendous sin, God would run to meet him if he would turn to Him; the Lord is not willing that any should perish.[61] I wrote that hell was not prepared for man, even though there are horrible criminals there, but rather it was made for the devil and his servants.[62] With that, I sent him this letter.

From that moment on, we began to correspond. He had many questions, and we exchanged letters almost every day. The re-investigation of his case continued, and this was followed by a new trial. All told, my correspondence with him went on for about four months. Once the trial had begun, he returned from court and wrote that, even though the case had been re-opened, he could already tell that it would not change his fate. Rather, the trial would only serve to condemn yet another of his accomplices to execution.

When the trial was approaching its climax and another sentencing, very early in the morning about five a.m. (reveille was at 6), the prisoners began knocking from the cell beneath us, and we received a letter. In prison-speak, we would say, "the pony has arrived." So we took the pony into the stable, and as I began to read, this man Peter was writing to tell me that that very night he had surrendered his heart to the Lord. He had believed God's truth, and the Lord had come into his life. Now he no longer had any fear and had rejoiced all night, not being able to sleep for joy. He had written this letter and couldn't even wait for reveille but had to send it right away.

I gave thanks to the Lord, and understood that it was for the sake of this one horrible sinner God had allowed me to experience these things and be put in this awful cell. God protected me here, and that man who had totally had his way with the other two men in the cell didn't so much as lift a finger against me. God then took this man out of the cell and fulfilled His plans to save the other prisoner through my words. I rejoiced in this,

---

61 2 Peter 3:9 "The Lord is not slack concerning his promise, as some men count slackness; but is longsuffering to us-ward, not willing that any should perish, but that all should come to repentance."

62 Matthew 25:41 "Then shall he say also unto them on the left hand, Depart from me, ye cursed, into everlasting fire, prepared for the devil and his angels…"

that these sufferings were not in vain, and that even here in prison people accepted Christ: that His Word found fertile ground where it might abide and bring forth fruit.[63]

It turned out that the second day after his repentance, he sent me another letter. In this letter he made an appeal to all youth involved in the sins of unbelief, perversion and crime. It was a disturbing letter. He implored me, "Brother Peter, you keep this letter safe, and when you are set free…I don't know what will happen to me: I will probably be sentenced to death again…But as soon as you are free, publish this letter. May it be an eye-opening account for all those young people whose lives are threatened with becoming involved in the same sins and unbelief that I once knew."

I thanked God that He was working in the heart of this man, and although I tried to keep this letter I was unable to do so. Unfortunately, when I was transferred from Chita to a political zone[64] in Perm Oblast in the Urals, I was forced to dispose of it. The soldiers had already taken all my letters and notes from me once, and when they gave it back I decided that I had to destroy it. When I arrived at this zone, I saw that I had done the right thing, because here they took not only whatever notes I had on me, but also all pieces of paper: envelopes, letters, blank sheets—absolutely everything; and I never got any of these things back.

---

[63] John 15:5 "I am the vine, ye are the branches: He that abideth in me, and I in him, the same bringeth forth much fruit: for without me ye can do nothing."

[64] political zone: A prison camp complex for political prisoners.

CHAPTER TWENTY

SOMETIME AROUND THE END OF October 1986, I was finally sent off to be transferred to another facility. This was a very arduous transfer process as we were travelling through various facilities: I went through the hard labor prisons of Novosibiirsk, Sverdlovsk and Perm. Finally I ended up in the zone. There were many things that happened as I was being transferred. When they transferred me from Chita to Novosibiirsk prison, they gave me back my Bible that had been sitting in storage for about six years there. I read it with great thirst as the other prisoners were sleeping in the compartment. The guard in the corridor looked through the peephole into the compartment once, then twice, then opened the feed slot. At this, a woman's voice—this was a female guard—called to me and said, "What are you reading?"

I said, "I'm reading the Word of God. I have a Bible."

She replied, "Listen, do you think you could let me borrow it to read for a little while? Things are going to stay pretty quiet around here until lunch time, and nobody will bother me until then."

"It would be my pleasure!" I said, and gave her the Bible. She read it for about an hour and a half, and then, when everyone was asleep once more, she quietly came up to return the Bible. She opened the feed slot, and we got into a small discussion. She told me that there was a group of Baptists that met not far from where she lived. I replied that she should somehow hook up with that group and go to their services, and she promised that she would do so.

Of course, the devil didn't like this at all, that not only could I feed on the Word of God, but that other people—even among the guards—were also able to read the Word. It was then that he decided to make his attack against me: our cell was searched while we were having exercise time in the yard one day. When I returned, no one else had had anything taken from them, but my Bible had disappeared from my bag. I informed the cell-block commander of this, and demanded in earnest that they return my Bible to me. They answered that they would set things in motion to get the Bible back to me, but about an hour later the block commander came to me and said that they would not return it. I replied, "Then, give me a receipt saying that you've confiscated my Bible." He replied that no such receipt would be given, and I understood that they intended to take the Bible from me for good. I began thinking about what I should do next. It was clear from the way that they had taken it in this shifty, round-about fashion that they intended to destroy it. Then I indicated that I would not relent in demanding to get the Bible back. Furthermore, I said that I would not leave the cell—even if they came to transfer me to another prison—until they gave the Bible back. And as it turned out, soldiers came that very evening to transfer me to another prison. When the soldiers came to take me with the other prisoners to the train, I indicated my demands, that my Bible had been taken from me in this fashion and that I would go nowhere until it was returned to me. The brigade commander refused to take me with the others, so they took me back to the cell.

The next day, the assistant warden called me in to his office. In furious anger he threatened me, saying that the Bible was a book that didn't correspond to reality, that no Bible could exist in a country where Communism was being built, that "we are waging a battle against this." And then he added, "Therefore, you will not get your Bible back."

"No," I replied. "You are obligated to return my Bible to me." I spoke to him boldly and outright, but he was yelling at me the whole time. I cut him off and said that, as a lieutenant colonel[65] and a professional military man, a so-called "steward of the regime," it was unacceptable for him to behave in this fashion.

He replied, "I'm going to put you in the hole now, and you're going to stay there for as long as we feel like it."

Everything really did seem to be pointing in the direction that they really would put me in the hole. The colonel pressed a button, at which point some guards came to take me away. Instead of putting me in the hole, though, they put me in a small holding cell we called the "cool-off tank." There was only room for one person in this cell, and there was a small bench where I could sit down. I was in this cell for about an hour. I was praying and wondering, "What happens now?"

The guards came back and took me back in to the Lt. Colonel. As I walked in, I saw my Bible laying on his desk. There was also a lieutenant in the room with him. When I entered, the commandant asked, " Is this your Bible?"

"It's mine."

He replied, "The lieutenant here was involved in the search where it was siezed. I gave the order for them to find it and return it. Here, I'm returning your Bible to you." Then to the lieutenant he said, "You're dismissed."

With that, we were left alone. Our discussion now continued in a completely different fashion. The Lt. Colonel asked questions about several passages from the Scriptures. It turned out that he had a grandmother who was a Baptist, and this grandmother had spoken to him a great deal and encouraged him that he needed to accept Christ and receive God's truth.

---

65 In the Soviet Union and modern Russia, all prisons are administered by military personnel. The warden of a prison holds the rank of colonel, and his subordinates hold the appropriate military ranks. (Thus, the rank of the administrator directly subordinate to the warden is "Lt. Colonel.") There is, in fact a deeper distinction revealed here between the American and Soviet systems, in that the American system maintains a stricter separation of police powers: Soldiers are not used as police, covert and investigative operations within the United States cannot be carried out by the CIA., etc. (That is, in the US, the CIA's charter stipulates that intelligence gathering be directed outside the United States. [Though this would exclude inter-departmental operations.] Internal investigations are handled by the FBI and other organizations. In the Soviet Union, the State Security Committee [KGB] filled multiple police functions, combining the FBI, CIA and other services into one branch.) With the fall of the Soviet Union, the KGB was renamed the FSB or, "Federal Security Service."

He was a completely different person. I understood that the Lord through my prayers was working in his heart and had laid it on his heart to return my Bible. We had a great conversation there for about an hour—maybe more—and when we parted company we exchanged warm wishes with each other.[66] He wished me a successful return home, and that my God on Whom I relied would help me to serve out my sentence, adding the wish that I might even be paroled early. (Of course, he had no idea as to whether I would be set free early or not, just as I didn't. These were nothing more than friendly wishes.) Nonetheless, I thanked him for such a warm desire, and in turn said that God was waiting for him to surrender his heart to Him. That God loved him and gave His Son Jesus Christ for him. So we parting by shaking hands. Of course, it was not allowed for prisoners to shake hands with the officers, but he was the first to extend his hand to me, and I understood that here it was O.K.

---

[66] Since this seems to be a more codified tradition in the Soviet Union than in the U.S., it bears commentary that it is customary among friends in Russia to wish each other well when parting company for an extended time (or parting company for good). It is significant here, because it would be very unusual for a prison official to bestow good wishes on an inmate.

CHAPTER TWENTY-ONE

I WAS SOON TRANSFERRED AND sent to the prison at Sverdlovsk. This was one of the worst transfer prisons that existed at that time in the entire Soviet Union. I had to go through this prison four times, and each time the conditions changed progressively for the worse. The last time I had been there, they didn't even give mattresses to the prisoners being transferred. (If they had given us mattresses before, then they were "mattresses" in name only. In actuality, these were bags with a little bit of fluff that still hadn't quite been smashed out of them with a pillow in the same beat up condition. These bags were filthy through and through, and the inmates used to say that a hundred men had already died on them before you got one.) That was the kind of bedding they gave us, but this last time they didn't even give us that.

I was expecting all these horrors to be repeated. The last time I had been there for a total of two weeks, and it had been extremely cramped. When our train stopped and they began to take us out for transfer from the station to the prison, we were removed from the car one at a time. The convoy conductor was behind us there in the corridor. When my turn came, I grabbed my bag with my things in it. The conductor was walking behind me. The door to the car was open, and I looked out to see soldiers standing there with machine guns and dogs. The prisoners who had already left the car were sitting on their coats beside the car.

Suddenly, there was a blow to my back, and I went flying out of the car. There was a ditch directly outside the car, and I fell in such a way that I could feel that my left leg had been seriously injured. I pulled myself out of the ditch and stood up, but I was unable to walk on that leg. They ordered me to sit on my coat, and as I did, I noticed that they were sending other people flying into the ditch just as they had done to me. The soldiers at this time were standing menacingly over us with their machine guns, and they said to us, "If we could, we'd not only shoot you, but we'd let these dogs tear you to pieces!" In this, the soldiers were just dripping with all the hatred that they had been taught.

Seeing all this hatred that they harbored against us, I prayed to the Lord that He would somehow work in their hearts. We still had to walk a long way to the vehicle that was going to take us to the prison, but I was unable to walk. Nonetheless, they continued pressing us to hurry up. Two of the prisoners in the convoy took me by the arms to help me along; really, they just carried me across the tracks. I finally made it to the transport with great difficulty.

They were putting so many people in the car that there was already no room for us. Now, I wasn't the last one to be put in, but the soldiers pushed the last ones in with their feet because there was nowhere for them to go. When they finally began to close the door, the last two prisoners' feet were still outside, and the soldiers nearly broke them as they attempted to slam the great metal door shut. They screamed terribly; we all screamed. Finally, they took a few of the prisoners out and sent us on our way.

When we arrived at the prison, I asked to see the doctor, to whom I explained the whole situation. I also demanded that the prosecutor[67] get involved in this affair. I thought that my leg was probably broken, though it turned out not to be. They took me immediately to get a shower, and one of the prisoners came to get my personal belongings and the mattress they gave me. They also gave me a sort of cane, and I used this to walk with great difficulty to the cell to which I was led. This was an isolation cell. Since it was already the month of October, the cell was very cold, but I noticed that the radiator was warm. I laid out my mattress, and they had even given me sheets (a top sheet and a cover sheet)—They had even been laundered, and were thoroughly cleaned. I even had a pillow.

I got down on my knees and thanked God: I understood that if this had not have happened, I would have been put back in the common cell with the others—where it was crowded, where there were bedbugs everywhere,

---

[67] In the American judicial system, this would be a rough equivalent to the "District Attorney."

where the room was so filled with smoke that you couldn't even see the people in front of you. But here I was in isolation. I had a Bible. I read the Word of God and prayed again, and soon I forgot about the pain in my leg—for the doctor had bandaged it up tightly. I fell asleep. How long I slept, I don't know, but it was a long time. I didn't hear when they brought in lunch, but I awoke when they knocked again to bring dinner. I ate, then read the Word of God some more, rejoicing at how God works.

In the evening, I talked with the guard through the feed slot. Since there was only this one cell on the corridor, he had gotten really bored sitting out there by himself. I talked to him a great deal about God, how God wanted this man to come to Him. I opened God's truth to him. God worked in my heart such that, wherever I was: in prison, in the zone, being transferred—God gave me the strength and desire to witness to everybody, inmates and guards alike, about that wonderful and miraculous love that the heavenly Father had revealed to us through His Son Jesus Christ. More than once, the inmates and prison officials alike would ask, "Why, then, if you have such a loving God, and He really loves you so much...Why does He allow you to be here with us, so that you suffer, your family suffers... Why is it like that if you have such a loving God?"

I answered the prisoners that, under other circumstances, they wouldn't want to hear about God, so I was here to tell them about Him. I told the prison officials, on the other hand, that I was here to be an example and a testimony for them so that they might accept Christ.

Of course, I understood that God allows suffering in our lives to try our faith and to see to just what extent we are surrendered to our Lord,[68] so that these sufferings would be like a fire to purify us so that we might come forth as gold tried by fire.[69] I never doubted my God as He allowed these things to happen to me. I knew that all this served for my benefit and prepared me for my life with Him in heaven. I thank Him for all that.

---

[68] Romans 5:3–5 "...but we glory in tribulations also: knowing that tribulation worketh patience; and patience, experience; and experience, hope: and hope maketh not ashamed; because the love of God is shed abroad in our hearts by the Holy Ghost which is given unto us."

[69] I Peter 1:7 "That the trial of your faith, being much more precious than of gold that perisheth, though it be tried with fire, might be found unto praise and honour and glory at the appearing of Jesus Christ..."

CHAPTER TWENTY-TWO

I WAS FINALLY TRANSFERRED TO Perm Prison. There I was put in isolation. The discipline at Perm was very strict. At six a.m. reveille, the prisoners had to put up their mattresses, and no one was allowed to lay back down before convocation. They were allowed only to sit: there was a wooden bench and a table that could be used for writing or eating.

The long days of isolation dragged on. I had a Bible with me, for as I already said, they gave this Bible back whenever I was transferred from one prison to another. They wanted to put it in storage when I arrived, but I didn't agree to that, and they let me keep it with me in the cell. For a while, I wondered why they were keeping me in isolation without any other prisoners in the cell.

About a week after I had been there, the door was opened early one morning, and a new prisoner entered. His name was Alexander. I could see that he was an educated man, an economist by profession. He had graduation from the Lekhanov Economic Institute in Moscow and worked as an economist. He and his wife had desired to leave the Soviet Union, but they were always denied tourist visas. Every time he tried to go to another country, it was just impossible for him to get a visa.

So he decided to hijack a plane and fly to Sweden. And that's what they did: He and his wife agreed on the matter, and they boarded a plane in Riga bound for Leningrad. Once in the air, his wife went up to the pilot and demanded that they change course for Sweden. She showed them where her husband was sitting back in the cabin, and as they looked back, he raised the hand resting on his bag to reveal a bomb with his other hand on the trigger. She said, "If you don't change course for Sweden, my husband back there is going to blow us all to smithereens." The pilots didn't argue with them and changed course for Sweden. When they were within sight of Sweden, the plane dropped altitude and landed, but it landed not in Sweden, but on an island just off the coast. This island was what you could say was the very last bulwark of Soviet territory, and it was controlled by Soviet border troops. No sooner did the plane land but the border guards burst into the cabin and discovered that there was no explosive device in the bag. Both this man and his wife were arrested and tried: He was sentenced to 15 years in prison for betrayal of the motherland, and his wife was given five years as an accomplice.

This man and I had discussions about God. He, of course, was not a believer, and he was very bitter about all that had happened to him. He said to me, "If there is a God, then He wouldn't have done this to me. I'm not a bad man, I just didn't like our political system. There was no way for me to change it, and it didn't work out when I tried to escape. And if there is a God as you say that would allow all these sufferings, then I cannot believe in God."

Obviously, this was a very difficult man whose heart was as the stony ground that would not accept the seed of salvation.[70]

We were there for about a week and a half before they transferred us to the zone. This time we were sent from Perm Prison to an area containing three penal zones located in a sort of triangle. In the center of this triangle sat the village of Skalnya, from which the local office of the KGB ran the three political zones. I was sent to one of these zones.

When I arrived, I was put in one of the isolation cells. Normally, prisoners were not given a mattress, or blanket, or anything to wear on their feet and heads. Prisoners were usually put in these cells as a form of punishment, but since I hadn't done anything meriting punishment, they gave me bedding, and I had my personal belongings with me as well as two prisoners' coats, warm clothes, warm socks and boots, and a winter hat. It was cold and dank in this cell. There was a slimy precipitation that ran down the wall, and I cleaned it off daily to prevent having a big mess

---

[70] That is, where the Word falls by the way side. Mark 4:15 "And these are they by the way side, where the word is sown; but when they have heard, Satan cometh immediately, and taketh away the word that was sown in their hearts."

on the floor. I sat all day long wrapped up in these coats and hat with the ear-flaps down. At night I would lay wrapped in the sheets with these coats still on and the flaps still down.

Every day, somebody from the prison administration would come: either someone from the warden's office or one of the lower-ranking officers, and the doctor would come. I asked all of them why they where keeping me in isolation, and they answered, "You were in transit for a long time, so you have to go through quarantine here in isolation. During quarantine, if you've brought in any infectious diseases they will most definitely manifest themselves during this time. If it turns out that you don't have any diseases, then we'll release you from isolation in about two weeks into the zone." They had an additional, ulterior motive, however, in coming to me, which was to ask me how I planned to conduct myself here: "Would I pray openly?" "Was I going to witness to others about the Lord and Savior Jesus Christ?" I answered affirmatively, to which they replied, "If that's how you're going to act, then you will sit in this cell indefinitely." In other words, they were showing me what it was like in the cell here so that I could evaluate it. Would I comport myself as God wanted me to, confessing Him before others without shame or fear of the reactions of men? Or would I get scared and keep quiet—stop praying and stop telling others about God?

Finally, they released me into the zone. This was during the day time, and I could see that the living conditions here were better than in the other areas where I had been during my 17 years of imprisonment. Here the grounds were kept, and there were screens on the windows. The guard showed me where I could bunk and where I could get bedding, then said, "Get yourself set up." I went to get my mattress and sheets, and when I returned with them, the other prisoners where returning from work for lunch. When they saw me, we began to exchange greetings and get acquainted. And when they found out I was a Baptist, they met me with joy, saying, "Here we haven't had a single new prisoner come to us in a year, and here we get one—and he's a Baptist!"

There were several questions that interested them. Since they already knew that there existed such a thing as the underground church, it was clear to them that I must be from this underground church. And was there really a Christian press? They had heard of a Christian press that was publishing Testaments, Bibles, hymns, journals...They had also heard of the Council of Prisoners' Relatives. So they asked how that work was going and whether they had already arrested everybody involved in this printing. Of course, there was a lot that I didn't know about all this, since I had been in prison for six years. But whatever I could learn from my wife during visitation I passed on to them, and they were happy to hear it.

Life here got off on a different foot, and the relations between the prisoners were different. This was polite society.[71] I could still see clearly, however, that a man without God could never be happy no matter who he was—convict, criminal or a member of polite society. Without God there is no happiness, for all people need the truth of God's salvation.

These people didn't especially take to accepting God's truth. They had their own interests. I also saw that every one of these people considered himself smarter than all the rest. The ground was always ripe for debate, and they could argue about any subject for days on end, especially when we had a day off.

When they sent me to work, they gave me the hardest job: we put together assemblies for an electric iron comprised of nine separate parts. I remember it as if it were yesterday, how I was supposed to make 830 of these assemblies. I had to work very quickly to make this quota, and there was no room for error. If any of the assemblies should turn out defective, then we were punished severely for the waste of parts. The idea behind all of this was that I wouldn't be able to make the quota, giving the administration the excuse it needed to put me in the hole. The devil had it in mind for them to put me in the hole for my failure to fill the quota.

The work was so tiring that it was absolutely exhausting, but there was still no way for me to fill the quota. But God worked in the hearts of the others. There were ten work stations involved in this operation, and toward the end of the shift the others would come up to me. They had already been working at this a long time, so they were able to meet their quotas a half-hour or so before the shift ended. They would come up to me and ask how many pieces I still had to assemble to make my quota. Then one would make perhaps 10 more, another 15, and in this way they would make sure that I made the quota. This meant that the administration couldn't throw

---

[71] The inmates in this prison were almost entirely comprised of the educated "upper class": political thinkers and dissidents.

me in the hole. All the same, this was very degrading work, and I developed high blood pressure from the stress of it. God was aware of all this, however, and soon I was switched to an easier job.

One morning, I got up, washed and got myself in order, then knelt down and began to pray. At that moment, I heard someone yell my last name. I went to breakfast, and after breakfast someone came to take me to the administration. I came in to the colony commander's office, and he asked, "Did you pray today?"

I replied, "Yes, I prayed today. But not just today: I pray every day."

"Didn't we tell you that if you prayed we would put you in the hole? And this morning you didn't respond when the guard called your name...."

"I heard someone call out my name this morning," I said. "But I was praying at the time to the Chief Administrator of all administrators, to God, the Creator of all the universe. I was unable to respond to the yell. And besides that, I didn't know it was the guard."

"Because you prayed today in direct disobedience to the administration, we're going to put you in the hole."

They already had an act prepared, in which it was detailed that, in violation of their order, I had prayed openly. It was also required for me to sign the act, in effect saying that I agreed with the charges and the punishment. I said, "I will sign this act only if you allow me to note my motives and my opinion on the matter of what you intend to do with me."

"No," they replied, "no explanations are necessary here. Sign it, and that's all!"

"No," I replied, "I refuse to sign."

So they called the guards, and they signed the act. "Today we're going to put you in the hole," I was told.

I thought back to that horrible cell I had been in before for 12 days. At that time, however, they had given me warm clothes: I had two warm coats, and I had a mattress...But now I was going to be in the cell with only a light coat. My heart was very heavy at the thought of this, of course. I thought that any moment they would come to put me in that cell, but instead I was taken away to work with the others.

As I was working up until lunch time, I was expecting them to come for me at any moment. However, we worked right up to when the bell sounded for lunch. At that moment, one of the officers walked up to me and said, "Let's go." I was thinking that they were now going to throw me in the hole, but instead they took me to another room where the lieutenant commander of the colony was sitting.

He began our interview by asking whether I was a specialist at repairing boilers.

"Yes," I replied.

"We've looked over everybody's documents, you see, and discovered that you are a specialist qualified to repair boilers. Here in this zone, we have only politicals and white-collar people, meaning that nobody else has the professional skills to repair boilers." He then proceeded to explain what had happened: "Last night, one of the main boilers went out. (The system was comprised of two main boilers and two smaller, back-up boilers.)[72] This morning, the second main boiler went out. So we switched to the two smaller-powered boilers. For one thing, these two boilers are now being used to heat the entire zone—all the apartments, and the officers' and soldiers' quarters—and there's very little heat in these buildings. Secondly, the temperature outside is dropping steadily. (It was already about –50° C).[73] If these last two boilers go out, then we'll all freeze to death, prisoners, soldiers and officers alike. So you go eat lunch double quick, and then there's another old man who has some idea of how to fix these things. You guys get together and get one of those main boilers operational as soon as you can!"

As I left his office, I praised God, for I had clearly seen His hand. These people had intended to kill me off in a cold isolation cell, but here God had dropped the temperature to take out these boilers, so the tables were turned. I began working on these boilers. I prayed openly during this time and openly told others about God, but for the two weeks that we were working on these boilers no one so much as laid a finger on me.

As soon as we had finished the repairs on the boilers, I was brought that same day in to the administration along with somebody else. They had us

---

[72] Russian architectural regulations are distinct in this regard from American codes. Large central boilers are used for the heating needs of several buildings, as opposed to the American system which uses individual boilers for each individual building. The result is that, as indicated here, all the buildings depend on a single heating system.

[73] 58 degrees Fahrenheit below zero.

strip down below the waist as if we were being searched for something, but this was just to degrade and humiliate us. When they brought me in, they said, "Now, we have an act here that says we need to put you in the hole, but that would be a violation of proper protocol on our part to which the prosecutor might protest. So for the time being, we won't put you in the hole. Consider yourself warned, though: if you continue to pray and talk to other people about God, then our next step will be to put you in the hole. For now, we will simply take away your right to receive your next parcel. (That is, I was allowed to receive a parcel of up to 5 kg once a year for each year that I was incarcerated.) So they were already taking that parcel from me in advance, and they also took my right to buy anything in the canteen. (There, we were allowed to buy five rubles worth of foodstuffs.)

So they told me that I would be put in the hole if I prayed. I nonetheless relied on God and believed that, whatever happened, God would not allow me to die in that cold punishment cell. If God could protect Daniel in the lions' den, if He could keep the three friends Shadrach, Meshach, and Abednego in the fiery furnace, then He could protect me in this cold cell as well.

For about a week after that, they would call me in with another prisoner after work. (There was also a Catholic clergyman there in the prison.) We would be strip-searched, and after letting us stand there for a while they would tell us to get dressed and leave. There was talk among the other prisoners that some especially harsh order must have come down concerning us for them to be treating the religious prisoners this way.

In this zone, I was deprived of all correspondence. Not only were all the letters I wrote confiscated, but they also confiscated all the letters from home written by my wife and children. Almost daily, I became more and more acquainted with the camp's censor act. The censor would send me a notice that I had received a letter or two letters, but that they were confiscated for whatever reason or other that they had thought up.

Eventually, they called me in to talk to the KGB operative. (The guard was handled by the MVD: the Ministry of Internal Affairs, which was under the control of the KGB. The KGB man didn't involve himself in the daily operations of the camp, but he would sometimes call prisoners in to speak with him.) So one day he asked me to come in. I told him that I wouldn't speak to him; that is, I told him, "I'll talk to you about God, but there is nothing further for us to discuss." I knew that he was going to ask questions designed to entrap me. At this point, the conversation changed drastically, and they tried to put me in the hole. God kept that from happening, however.

CHAPTER TWENTY-THREE

ONCE AFTER WORK AN OFFICER came up to me that I hadn't seen before and said, "Let's go." I didn't know where. The system was set up so that whenever someone from the administration took you somewhere, you didn't know where you were going until you arrived. We started off in the direction of the hole, but then they took me on into the barracks and told me that I had fifteen minutes to collect my things, that I was then going to be sent away for transfer. When I went in, there was an old man in the barracks who had accepted Christ while I was there. He told me that I was the fourth that day to be transferred, and that three were already in the holding cell awaiting transfer. I gathered my things, and as I walked in, I saw that I was the fourth, just as he had said. Other prisoners were added to this number from other barracks, after which we were loaded onto a transport and taken to the train station.

When they let us out at the station, I saw that the conditions were completely different from what they normally would have been. Usually, there was a very strict guard here with dogs and machine guns. Here, however, the soldiers were armed only with pistols; no machine guns were to be found. The colonel commanding them was also armed only with a pistol, and there were no dogs. None of the men from the prison administration were here. After dividing us up into two groups of four (there were eight prisoners in all), they had us board.

As I got on the train, I saw that this was not the kind of car normally used to transport prisoners. I had expected this to be a standard prison car, but as I got on, I saw that it was just an average sleeper car. Several of the compartments were open, and I could see civilians sleeping there. They took the four of us to an empty compartment, and the Lieutenant Colonel and several sergeants sat down with us. Then the colonel said, "Keep your voices down and don't make any noise; there are people sleeping in the car, and you can see that you're being transported in a civilian train. Last night we received an urgent telegram ordering us to use whatever form of transportation necessary to get you on your way to Perm prison by morning, so now that's what we're doing."

We had a journalist from Kiev with us, and he wrote all of this down. He commented, "These are all really big changes that we're seeing. They'll probably take us on in to Perm prison in Volgas!"[74] Of course he turned out to be wrong. They took us to the prison in the same sort of van in which we had come to this station. But we were received in a completely different fashion when we arrived at Perm prison than when I had come there before as a transferee from Chita.

The prison officials here, for one thing, were more accommodating: I had been given the chance to go to the canteen before we left, and there I had bought ten cans of fish. When we arrived at Perm, I had to hand these over for storage, since we were not allowed to keep them in the cell. I responded that I would give them over into storage only if I could be permitted to retrieve one each day thereafter. They answered that I would not be allowed to go to storage that often, at which point I asked, "Then I request that you allow me to keep these cans with me in the cell." They appealed my request all the way up to the warden, with the result that they allowed me to keep them with me. This was just one of several instances where it was clear that they were being nicer to us than usual.

There were four of us in the cell. We slept for a while, and then they brought us lunch. After that, the warden of the prison, his assistant and the prison's doctor came in to see us. They asked us several questions, and the warden asked whether we were getting any newspapers here in the cell. We answered, "We are only allowed to get the regional newspapers, as you already know."

He said, "The people from the prison library are going to come now, and you will be able to take whatever books and newspapers you want to

---

[74] Volga: A Soviet-manufactured passenger sedan, considered to be the finest quality. Culturally, this would be the equivalent of the American Cadillac.

read." Then they came, and they had a huge stack of newspapers, representing almost all the major newspapers that were printed at that time in the Soviet Union. They offered us books to read.

The second day, they brought us breakfast in the morning. This wasn't the standard faire, however. Instead, they brought us special dietary rations. This was better than the normal faire, and was reserved for those prisoners who were sick. Of course, they were basically "special" rations in little more than name only, but they were better than what the regular prisoners got. We returned this food and said, "You've made some kind of mistake. We're not on special rations. Please take these back to those who are on the rations."

In a few moments, though, the cell-block commander came and told us, "No, these are *your* rations." At that point we understood that they were trying to get us in shape physically and improve our appearance.

After lunch, they began calling us in one at a time. I was also brought in to another area of the prison, where I noticed that the standard regiment had been altered: Normally, the prisoners were bound and not allowed to speak, but here the commander himself began talking to me, asking me questions.

"What do you think, why have they brought you here?" he inquired.

"I don't know," I said. "You're the one who should be telling me."

"To be honest, I don't know either."

And this was the honest truth. They didn't know why we had been brought here. We entered another block, where the captain knocked at the door and, as they opened it, called me to follow him. Here we were standing in a beautiful office with brass fixtures, and a prosecutor was sitting there with many stars decorating his uniform. He warmly invited me to sit down, and he began to explain that he had carefully studied my file and found that I had been sentenced unjustly. He continued that, concerning myself and my cellmates, the Presidium of the Soviet Union had already passed the preliminary draft of an act granting us our freedom.

I asked, "Do you mean to say that there is already a presidential order for our release?"

"No," he said. "There is not yet a specific order, but in the very near future you are all going to be set free. And now the Party and the government would like to know if, when you are released, you intend to engage in any political activity?"

I answered, "I am not a politician, I am a Christian. I was sentenced for my activities as a Christian. Furthermore, you indicated that you were acquainted with my file, so you know that I never confessed to being any sort of activist, neither when I was free, nor when I was tried"

"Yes, I've noticed that to indeed be the case," he replied.

"I will, therefore, not be involved in politics once I am set free."

"Could you put that in writing for me?" he said.

"Yes," I replied.

He gave me a piece of paper, and I began to write a letter addressed to the Supreme Soviet of the USSR. He tried at first to dictate the contents, but I asked that he excuse me, in that I was quite capable of writing the letter without his help. I wrote that, since I had been sentenced unjustly, I therefore requested to be released. I wrote further that, as a Christian, I would not engage in any political activity, just as I had never engaged in any political activity before.

I handed the paper over to him, and as he read it, a shadow fell across his brow. He said, "Now, you shouldn't be making any requests in this letter."

I said, "I'm not making any requests. I'm innocent, and that means that they should set me free. What I have written, I have written."

He then asked whether I would want to be sent back home once released.[75] I replied, "My family always looks forward to the time when I return home. They'll take me in."

He then said, "Alright. You are dismissed."

Two weeks later, the same captain that had brought me in to see the prosecutor came again after lunch and took the four of us out of the cell. He said, "The Presidium of the Soviet Union has passed a resolution to set you free. If the main office can get all your papers in order by the end of the day, then you will be released by the end of the day. If not, then you will definitely be released tomorrow morning." It turned out that we were sent off on the morning of the following day. Of course, they took all the clothes

---

75 That is, he was given the opportunity to be sent to a new location after release to start his life anew if he wished.

that we had been wearing and had us change into new prison uniforms that they had brought from storage. This was done so that we wouldn't be able to smuggle out any sensitive information about the prison that we might have sewn into our clothing. They were in such a hurry to get us on our way, that they didn't even collect the pass that they had given me to get out of the compound. Once we were on the train, the officials bade us farewell, and we were on our way bound from Perm to Moscow.

On the way home, we made a ten minute stop, and I was able to run and post a telegram home to announce my impending arrival. When we arrived the next morning in Moscow, I saw that there were a great many friends and relatives who had come with flowers to greet me. There were perhaps 40 people there in all. The political prisoners who had been released with me were simply amazed at this, for no one was there to meet them. There were so many flowers, though, that I gave a bouquet to each of the prisoners so that they would also be in high spirits on the occasion that they were now free.

Chapter Twenty-four

Peter Rumachik still in prison clothing right after his release in 1987.

So I RETURNED HOME ON February 6, 1987. From that moment, true *perestroika*[76] began in our country. Genuine and full freedom came to our land. In that year, all the believers who had been sentenced for religious reasons—Baptists and those of other denominations alike—were set free.

My family didn't have any problem at all registering me.[77] Physically, I was very weak. Even the prison doctors had detected a plethora of diseases in me, including heart and kidney trouble, and I felt very weak. I had high blood pressure. But God worked in such a way that I was soon able to regain my strength, and I no longer felt the effects of these infirmities.

---

[76] That is, "true re-structuring" or "true re-building"

[77] In the Soviet system, convicts are restricted as to where they are allowed to live. The fact that the author was able to register without any difficulties indicates that his record had been wiped clean.

A time of much excitement was also beginning in the church. Other brothers in Christ returned who had been imprisoned for the faith. The authorities no longer came to our services to break them up; if they did come, then it was only to make public service announcements. The church rejoiced in what God had done. We began to have contacts with churches abroad as well.

People were starving for the Word of God, for spiritual sustenance. During the first years of *perestroika*, people were drawn to listen to the Word of God. There were thousands of worship services being held in the squares, cultural centers, factories... There was complete freedom to hold worship services, and many souls came to repent of

Peter Rumachik meeting his daughter Nadya at the train station after his release in 1987.

their sins, and the Church was filled with many new souls.

It must be said, nonetheless, that the Baptists were not ready to proclaim the gospel in these new circumstances. Humanly speaking, we could not foresee these changes, but God was in the middle of all of this, so that that which the Church had been praying for for so long came to pass came to pass without the shedding of blood. Many of God's children believed in times past that there would come a time when God would destroy the godless regime, [and here it had come to pass].

CHAPTER TWENTY-FIVE

NOT LONG AFTER ALL THIS, the church began to spread out. That is, we had started a church where we had many young Christian men and women, and it didn't take long for us to enact a program for establishing new churches.

I remember when we went to the first evangelizational service. This was in the central city for our *raion*, in Istra. The cultural center there seated somewhere between 350 and 400. It was Christmas. When the service began, I went up onto the platform to greet everyone with Christmas wishes, and I noticed that not only were the seats full, but the aisles were completely packed with people so that there was no way to get through. There must have been upwards of 500 people in the hall at that meeting. We had brought something on the order of 350, perhaps 400, New Testaments, and as we passed them out there were not enough for everyone. We had already assigned Christian workers for follow-up work in that area, and we told the people to come back the following Sunday and invite their friends who didn't have Bibles to come with them—since we would be passing out Bibles next time. Thus we began the evangelization in that area. Since then the church in Istra has outgrown itself to become two churches, and the original church has over 100 members. Having just celebrated its seventh year anniversary, Istra is now involved in a building program.

Since 1990, our church in Dyedovsk has been sending out its best young Christian brothers and sisters to found new churches, the result of which has been the formation of a whole association of churches in the area. We are not part of any union; these are independent churches, though we do have an association of churches bound in brotherhood.

There are various places where churches are being built even yet today. In Nahabino, one of my sons is laboring as a missionary to build a church there. The walls and roof are already up, and now there are only a few details left. In the city of Podolsk (in Moscow Oblast) the walls and roof have also been completed. In Istra, the foundation for the building has been laid.

As I'm writing this small book, the economic situation in our land is not an easy one. There is a great economic crisis going on, and it is hard to see what will happen in the near future. Of course, there are people in power who want there to be only one church—the Orthodox Church—in our country. There are even those who proclaim this desire openly.

Whatever happens, though, it will be that which God has ordained according to His plans. We understand the difficulties inherent in our situation, and we seek to do that which is pleasing to the Lord. We labor to carry the gospel to others and work according to the strength God has given us.

When *perestroika* began, we and many of our brothers and sisters in the churches with whom we are associated received aid from abroad, as well as free literature which we were able to freely distribute to those who desired it. Nowadays, practically every home has a Bible in it, whether they believe in God there or not, and Christian literature can be obtained at kiosks and bookstores. We rejoice and thank God for that.

The economic situation in our country is very difficult. This makes it impossible for us to carry out the construction of church buildings on our own. Our desire is to build one new church building each year in these places. So we have a great need for financial support.

Peter Rumachik with one of the members of
Pushkinskaya Church laying bricks for the building.

Therefore, I appeal to all Christian brothers and sisters who read this book, that your hearts would be moved to help us in our financial needs in building these buidlings and carrying forth the message of salvation. This is something you can do, and may the Lord open your hearts to that need.

I thank my God that He has extended my life and kept me, and that I have been free now for over ten years. I also thank Him that those illnesses that I suffered in prison don't affect me, even though they make themselves felt now and again. I'm not bedridden, but am still capable of doing something. Two years ago, we finished the building for our church. Our main auditorium seats about 350, and our church is full to overflowing. We have youth, and we have two choirs: both an adult and a children's choir. We have Sunday School. For all this, we are thankful to our Lord.

It is my hope that God will help me. The Lord has given me back my health. When I was released from prison, I didn't think I would be able to do the things I have done and the things I still do now in the church. I am currently the elder pastor of Dyedovsk Baptist Church at Pushkinskaya St. 1a. Praise be to our Lord for all things! Alleluia, amen.

Family picture in 1982 with
Peter Rumachik glued on
since they said he was
"with them always."

Pavel Rumachik wedding party picture in 1990.

Pavel Rumachik and Larisa
shorty after their wedding.

Pavel and Larisa Rumachik with their
children Yuliya, Anton and Vika.

92

During the years of persecution, believers had to meet secretly for worship, as seen in these rare photographs of underground meetings...

...in summer...

...in winter...

...in rain.

Pavel Rumachik and BIEM staff member Chris Lovelace on the Arbat, a famous pedestrian promenade in central Moscow. The painted tiles in the background comprise the "Wall of Peace" that was erected under Gorbachev's Perestroika.

It was here that Pavel was able to fulfill his wish of becoming an evangelist as he and several other young men began an active program of street evangelism in 1987. This resulted in the formation of a young church that at the time of this writing continues to meet faithfully.

The many years Pastor Rumachik spent in prison have adversely affected his health. Here his son Pavel is visiting him in the hospital, and young Anton looks on as his grandfather shares wisdom from the Scriptures.

Luba Rumachik, holding an infant, with her six children in 1972 while Peter Rumachik was imprisoned.

From its difficult beginnings under persecution in 1956, the Lord has blessed the church in Dedovsk with tremendous growth, as seen here in the packed auditorium on this Sunday morning in 1996.

In this cultural center, Pastor Rumachik was tried and convicted for the faith five times...

...It is now the meeting place of this body of believers established through God's blessing on the labors of his son Pavel and brother-in-law Victor Smirnov.

The years of difficulty are not enough to keep Brother Peter out of the pulpit, just as he is seen here addressing the congregation at Dedovsk where he remains the senior pastor.

95

Vasily Smirnov, father of Luba Rumachik, is seen here fervently exhorting the congregation he labored with the Rumachiks to found over 30 years before. Not long before the time of this writing, Brother Vasily went on into eternity to spend his days with the Savior for Whom he also suffered faithfully in bonds.

Following the example of his father, Aleksei Smirnov now serves as pastor of Pushkinskaya Church with Brother Peter Rumachik.

Pastor Peter, wife Luba and son Pavel with BIEM Director Dr. Sam Slobodian (left to right) display the *samovar* and *matryoshka* dolls that have come to symbolize their culture.

Peter Rumachik with BIEM staff member Chris Lovelace, who served as his interpreter during this visit to the United States in 1998.

Peter Rumachik and Luba Rumachik with flowers in 1997.

Dyedovsk church meeting in the snow in 1987.

Immediately upon his release in 1987, Pastor Peter went back to openly proclaiming the Gospel.

Luba Rumachik clandestine meeting with Peter Rumachik in 1980 (snuck into Dyedovsk while exiled).

Luba Rumachik, age 17, with friend. (1954)

THE TESTIMONY OF
PAVEL RUMACHIK

"I HAVE BEEN YOUNG, AND now am old; yet have I not seen the righteous forsaken, nor his seed begging bread." These were the words of David in the 37th Psalm. I can fully attest to the righteousness of these words. I was young, very small, then I grew to become a young man, and finally now I am 34. In all that time that I have lived, I never saw a time that God forsook me or our family.

My name is Pavel Rumachik. I was born in the Moscow area. As the time of my birth was approaching, my mother and father were living in Siberia on the Angara River in Krasnoyarsk *Krai*. My father had been sent into exile there for the name of our Lord—for preaching the gospel—and that was where I was supposed to have been born. Nonetheless my mom went back to Moscow, and I was born there without my father being present. It's interesting to see how my mother checked herself into the maternity ward. It's interesting to see how her husband wasn't able to be there when she checked out. God did not forsake us, though. I was very big when I was born: nearly five kilograms[78] in weight. After I was born, my mother and I flew back to Krasnoyarsk *Krai* in Siberia where my birth certificate was issued. This made it so that I was officially registered as having been born in Siberia.

That's not a bad thing, though. It is a good sign and a good testimony of the fact that I was born into difficult circumstances, and that my life began in exile. This was, of course, significant for my father, but I also took part in what happened to my father. It's interesting that, from the time I was born until the time I was about 25, half of that childhood time I didn't see my father. And maybe somewhere that shows up in my life today: perhaps I don't have all the useful characteristics I would have picked up if he had been around. My mother reared me. But I am very thankful to God that He gave her such a good, strong character, and that He gifted her with the strength to rear the children, of which there were eight of us.

The Lord blessed our whole family. He blessed us not only in that we were able to serve Him, but also in that He gave us His gifts. I am

---

[78] Nearly 12 lbs.

Pavel Rumachik with sister Nadya in 1976.

especially thankful that He blessed us with the gift of music. In our childhood years when there was still a lot that we didn't understand, my sister Nadyezhda[79] and I would sing hymns and songs in two-part harmony. It was a great joy for us to praise the Lord and to serve Him in church. Even though we were without our father almost all the time, the Lord did not forsake us, but He supported and helped us.

It was very difficult for our mother to rear us. In 1961, our father was arrested, and for four years he was in exile. He was arrested as a *parasite*,[80] meaning that he didn't work, even though he *did* work, so that he was even working at the factory when they arrested him. Then when he was released from prison, he was only home for three years before he was again put in prison for a year and a half. He was let out of prison after that for a year and a half, then went back to prison for three years. He came back home for two years, then was imprisoned again for three years. Then they

---

[79] Nadyezhda: "Hope." Often shortened to "Nadya."

[80] The *parasite law* to which the author refers is an extension of the provisions of the Soviet Constitution of 1936: ARTICLE 118 sates, "The citizens of the U.S.S.R. have the right to work…The right to work is ensured by…the steady growth of the productive forces of Soviet society, the elimination of the possibility of economic crises, and the abolition of unemployment." Since individual unemployment was perceived as a threat to the Soviet economy as a whole, anyone not legally employed in a Soviet-sanctioned job could be tried as a criminal. ARTICLE 130 further stipulates, "It is the duty of every citizen of the U.S.S.R…to maintain labor discipline…" In the criminal codes of 1958 and 1960, this was actually codified into Article 209-1 of the RSFSR Criminal Codex, which provided punishment for "[t]he malicious evasion, by a person leading an anti-social form of life, of the performance of a decision of a district (or city) executive committee of a soviet [council] of working people's deputies concerning the arrangement of work and the discontinuance of parasitic existence…" This law was later relaxed to one year of incarceration rather than the four years of exile seen here. In effect, the *parasite law* said that there were no unemployed, only criminals, and it was used extensively to arrest those involved in the ministry, regardless of whether or not they were employed in state enterprises.

Pavel Rumachik, 1982, holding his violin. Before he was called to full-time ministry, Brother Pavel taught violin in Dedovsk.

gave him five more years. And so I spent practically my whole life without my father.

It was very difficult for our mother to rear all of us children, since the family was so large. Of course, the church showed concern for us and gave us the most essential aid. I don't remember any time that we were left hungry or cold, or that we didn't have something to wear. Sure, there were difficulties occasionally, but I am happy and thankful to God that He helped us. I do remember one time in particular when we didn't have anything to eat. Mom got down on her knees to pray with us, and we explained the situation: "Lord, You see that we don't have anything to eat…." No sooner had we gotten off our knees, but there was a ringing at the door. When mom opened it, there in the hallway stood a woman from the church with a bag of potatoes for us. This was a joyous blessing for all.

I remember how many believers showed their concern for us, and we would often receive small packages of food from Ukraine, from Belarus and from Russia, where the people of God shared with us what the Lord had given them. We would get candy (especially if it were some holiday like Christmas or Easter). We would get fruit (and the fruit was especially good that came from Moldavia). They would send honey, dried apples, even *seeds*, even *salo*.[81] Every time we would get one of these packages, we would rejoice for it as we knelt in prayer to thank God that He didn't forsake us, for *He* was our Father even though our father was in prison.

At the same time, the people around us were displeased that our family remained steadfast in the faith. There were all sorts of denigrations, revilings, rumors in our small city. The city of Dyedovsk, where I was born and where I now live, was a small town of some 40,000 inhabitants just outside of Moscow. People know each other there. People also know us, our family, because in the central Cultural Center the Lord allowed my father

---

[81] *Salo:* A type of salt-pork product that is highly prized in Slavic countries.

to stand trial as a "parasite of the people," and there he was able to testify to the people of the Truth. The people were very irate and enraged. The entire square in front of the cultural center was filled with people who were ready to tear these parasites to pieces who worked for America, and so on. How interesting to see how God worked, so that 30 years after my father was tried and sentenced for the name of Christ, the Lord allowed me, his son, to found a church, and we used that very auditorium where he was tried for preaching the gospel. My father himself, 30 years after being tried, was also able to preach the "words of eternal life"[82] there. How beautiful! This is the victory of our Lord, and it shows His strength and power. I am thankful to God that a church has been started there, and that to this day it serves God, worships Him, and praises His marvelous name. And even today sinners are coming there and finding salvation at His feet.

When I was 7 years old and in first grade, I went to school one day where I was informed that our oldest sister, the eldest daughter, had died. She died of kidney failure. This had something to do with malpractice on the part of the doctors, that they didn't detect the illness in time to keep the subsequent diseases from taking her life. I remember going to school that day, where they told me, "Your sister has died." When I went outside for recess to play with the other children, I already heard them saying, "Your mother sacrificed her daughter. Why did you do that to her?!" With each passing day, this just got worse and worse. Two or three days later, we had her funeral. Many guests came to share our loss with us, but our father was in prison at the time and could not be with us, since they would not release him for his eldest daughter's funeral.

When we went out on the day of the funeral, the whole city was filled with the rumor that "Baptists sacrifice their children, and here these Baptists have sacrificed their oldest daughter to God!" This was especially difficult for our mother to take, especially considering how much she had already endured. Not only had she had to deal with the death of her daughter, but now these fierce people were spreading this news that she had killed her. It's amazing that even today, some 30 years after my sister's funeral, there are still people in our city who believe that Baptists sacrifice

---

[82] John 6:68 "Then Simon Peter answered him, Lord, to whom shall we go? thou hast the words of eternal life." (In Russian, this verse reads: "…the verbs of eternal life…")

their children to God. Of course, I understand that this is due to ignorance, and I feel sorry for those people. But in some sense this interferes with people coming to services or coming to study the Bible. God, however, does not leave or forsake anyone.

■ ■ ■ ■ ■

THERE WERE SOME VERY SIGNIFICANT moments when we were studying in school. In our case, children were instilled with Communist ideals from the time they were young. When a child started first grade, then literally two months later at the beginning of November there would be a big convocation in which all the children would be inducted into the "Octobrists." The Octobrists were what we might call the "first disciples of Lenin." They were the "Octobrists" in honor of the October Revolution,[83] and these were children who desired to serve Lenin. At this time, each of the children was given a pin to wear on which the image of Lenin was imprinted.

As the children of Christian parents, we refused to participate in this. We said, "We cannot have any part in this, for it is a contradiction of our faith." Our parents would plead our case, as would we to whatever extent we were able. The school staff would pressure us a bit, but they weren't really tough on me in particular.

Then two years later in third grade, there was the second stage of faithfulness to Lenin's ideals and Communist principles. The students were inducted into the Pioneers on Lenin's birthday, the 22nd of April. Now the students didn't just wear little pins that could maybe go unnoticed, but they were dressed in red scarves reflecting the Soviet coat of arms. They would say to them, "BE PREPARED to defend Lenin's ideals!" And the Pioneers would answer back, "ALWAYS PREPARED!" Of course, we couldn't join that organization, and we didn't wear those scarves. There

---

[83] The "Great October Revolution" of 1917 actually occurred on November 7. At the time of the revolution, Russia was using the Julian calendar, which, because of its inadequacy in compensating for leap years, was two weeks behind the Gregorian calendar used in the West. Thus, the revolution occurred on October 25 in Russia, but is celebrated on the 7th of November. This difference in calendars is also apparent during Christmas: New Years Day falls on January 1, but Russian Christmas, reckoned by the old Orthodox calendar, falls on January 7.

were maybe one or two of us in the whole school that didn't wear these scarves, so we would be walking around like white ravens in the midst of a sea of red. Of course, neither the students, nor the teachers, nor the administration liked this very much. Sometimes it was difficult for us, and they would forcefully tell us to put on these scarves, because they would sit at the entrance to the school to check who was wearing their scarf and who was not. Whenever they saw that we weren't wearing ours, they would tell us to go home and put them on. Then our parents would have to come and explain that we couldn't participate in these organiza-

Three young pioneers can be seen sporting their red kerchiefs here in Odessa, 1989.

tions because they contradicted our faith. Of course, the school authorities were always actively trying to catch us in some sort of entrapment. Many times they would call me or one of us in from class to ask us questions. Often, these were investigators who were looking for evidence to convict my father or other believers. They would ask about things going on in the church and about who was involved in what. But our parents had taught us that, if they ever called us in to ask questions like this, we would just remain silent and say nothing so as not to be traitors. And that's what we did; we endeavored to be silent just as Christ was silent before Pilate, saying nothing.

Then in eighth grade, we experienced the next test of our faithfulness, since this was the time that children were inducted into the Komsomol.[84] Of course, we didn't join this organization either, and this set us apart from all the other students who joined the Komsomol (practically everybody else).

---

[84] Or, "Young Communist League"

So even from our earliest childhood, from the first grade[85] on, we felt pressure due to the fact that we did not pertain to this worldly, Soviet-Leninist movement. This was a good thing, though, because we were raised to realize that we were not part of this world or its system and viewpoints.

From the very beginning, our lives were intrinsically linked to the searches that were carried out in our home. Throughout the whole history of our family, we were searched over 15 times. What exactly do I mean by the term "search?" This is when KGB operatives or the police come into your home—and they have the right to take two of our neighbors as witnesses with them—and with a warrant in hand issued by the prosecutor's office, they search for literature and other paraphernalia designed to "topple Soviet power." The text of the warrant would be go something like this: "Be it known that this warrant is hereby issued for the purpose of detecting in the home of one Peter V. Rumachik all slanderous literature and other paraphernalia designed to overthrow the Soviet regime. et cetera, et cetera...." Under these auspices, anything was permissible. Quite honestly, we were not involved in politics in any way, nor did we have it in mind to topple the Soviet government as they claimed.[86] Speaking the Word of God in our services had nothing to do against flesh and blood, but under these auspices, they took all our Christian literature. They would come looking for Bibles; they would look for hymnals that we, the youth, had copied out by hand; they would take the poems that we would read in our services. This was very difficult for us to watch whenever they would find whatever we had, because we knew that they would confiscate it. Not only that, but we knew that someone from the family might be taken off to prison because of the literature. It was a sad thing to lose this literature,

---

[85] Kindergarten is not considered part of the scholastic program, but is more like "pre-school."

[86] The idea of "slander" ("the circulation of fabrications know to be false which defame the Soviet state and social system" or the preparation of such fabrications for distribution) was introduced into the Soviet criminal code (Articles 190-1, 190-3) on September 16, 1966 as a result of the famed show-trial of Soviet dissidents Andrei Sinyavsky and Yuli Daniel that began in February of that year. Respected dissident Vladimir Bukovsky is quoted as saying, " 'Slander' was a word that could be applied to everything the authorities didn't like." (as quoted by Tania E. Lozansky in her paper "The Role of Dissent in the Soviet Union since 1953." The Concord Review. 1996, date of authorship: 1989)

because 15 and 20 years ago, there was practically no literature being printed, and certainly none [like what we see nowadays] with a nice font face and quality binding. What was printed was done underground in difficult circumstances, and these materials were distributed by small groups moving from church to church. If anyone ever received a new piece of literature or perhaps a new hymnal, this was quite a joyous occasion.

I remember that the first Bible I ever got was the one I received at my baptism when I was 14. This was a very dear gift to me, since I didn't have a Bible, and I was overjoyed to receive this pocket-sized Bible. I was very thankful to God and the church. Whenever there were searches, I employed all possible means to save this Bible along with the other literature.

What did we do when they came to search our house? Since we had to protect and guard the literature in some way, we would try to hide it: while they were conducting the search in one room, we would be in another room finding all the literature we could and slipping in under our jacket or under our shirt so that it would just disappear from sight. Once they had finished searching one room, then all of us children would go back into the room they had just searched and hide the literature there that we had just grabbed. We'd try to put it back in the most obscure places possible: behind the bookcase, way up under the mattress, behind the trunk.... Of course, this was a scary moment, because we knew that, as we might be walking past one of these KGB agents, they could stop us at any moment and search us, catching us, as it were, "red-handed." Our love and desire to save this literature from these men, however, superceded any fear. As for the Bible that I was given, I was able to save through all the searches and persecutions, so that now it is with me even today. Now when I go to study at the seminary, I carry this Bible with me and use it to study. This is a very precious thing.

■ ■ ■ ■ ■

ONCE, I REMEMBER WHEN THEY came to search the house, and they knew exactly where the literature was. We knew that our home was bugged with listening devices, so we made every effort not to talk about the literature and where we had hidden it, or about any church-related matters.

Somehow, though, we gave away where the literature was, so that they went directly to the bathroom when they came to search us. There, as they searched for a long time, they discovered the literature that we had hidden behind the tub up against the wall. Also within this mass of documents, they discovered a large sum of money belonging to the church as well as many addresses and letters from believers (including addresses and letters from believers in America). And they confiscated it all!

After that, they went around to the other rooms looking for literature. At this time, our father was at home, and we understood that he was going to be taken into custody. The search began drawing to a close, and our mother started sewing a bag together for father so that he could take it with him to police headquarters. She put some warm clothes and food in the bag for him, and when the search was concluded, the police turned to him and just as we expected and said, "Peter Vasilevich, you must come with us to the station."

He replied, "What for?"

"We'll just detain you for a short time. Just long enough to clear up a few things, then you can return home," they answered.

But our father could see that they were lying, and he said, "Let me pray with my children first." The whole family went into the children's room, where we got down on our knees, and father prayed for blessings to be upon us and also on the path that lay before him now. All the while, the police were banging on the door to our room, saying, "Peter Vasilevich, that's enough! Cut it short!" Dad finished his prayer and hugged all of us goodbye. The police were saying, "Don't worry. Everything's going to be fine. You'll be coming right back home." With that, he left. And things did not turn out as the police had promised, but instead he was given three years in prison, and he returned home only after those three years were passed.

So we all knew quite well what a tough and frightening time this was, that because of a search, our father or somebody else might not come home again and could end up behind bars.

I remember another time when our parents were not at home. Mom had gone off somewhere as part of the ministry she had serving on the Council of Prisoners' Relatives. Our father was in prison. This made me the oldest child at home. Early in the morning, there was a ringing at the door. For some reason I had the innate sense that, if someone came calling early in the morning, then that meant it was the police coming to search us. Here it was some time around 7:00 or 6:30 in the morning, and someone was ringing the doorbell. I was the first to wake up, and the first thing through my mind was, "It must be a search!" I opened my eyes, got up, and tiptoed ever so quietly up to the door so that they wouldn't hear me. When I looked through the peephole, I saw men that I did not know standing in the corridor. I understood immediately that these were operatives—that is, people who had come from the police along with our neighbors to search the house. I backed away from the door on my tiptoes and began to hide all the literature on the shelves and in any other visible place. By this point, the ringing at the door had increased and become long and drawn out. Then they began to beat on the door, saying, "Open up! Open up!" I paid no mind to this as I continued to hide the literature, and the other children were still asleep. The blows became more and more forceful so that, finally, the door could not withstand this any more, and it flew off its hinges. At that, a whole gang of people—operatives, KGB and police together—came bounding in just as I managed to leave the room. When they saw me, they said gruffly, "Why didn't you open the door?!"

"Why'd you break it?!" I retorted. "What are you doing here?"

"We've come to search the house."

"Show me the warrant," I said. They showed it to me, and it turned they really were sanctioned to conduct a search. However, since I was the oldest one at home and still a minor, they couldn't search us because by law they could only conduct the search with a legal adult from the household present. This meant that they had to leave, which they did straightaway.

■ ■ ■ ■ ■

I REMEMBER ANOTHER TIME WHEN mom and dad weren't home, so I was left as the oldest to watch after the smaller children. A Christian sister came to us from the Urals to bring my mother documents about the persecutions that were going on there. These documents contained specific information about searches, pressure from the authorities, persecution, arrests. My mother worked on the Council of Prisoners' Relatives and often went to Moscow to send telegrams or make petitions for that the government to stop persecuting Christians. She sent telegrams to the Presidium and the Supreme Soviet, as well as abroad, and people came from all over the Soviet Union to tell my mother about whatever persecutions were going on so that she could then send off her telegrams.

So this woman came to bring information of that kind from the Urals.[87] It turned out that she had been followed, and it wasn't long after she arrived that I heard a ringing at the door. As I looked through the peephole, I understood immediately that these were activists and KGB. I turned to her and said, "What should we do?" In her bag, there were all sorts of documents relating to the persecutions. Should they come in to search us and find these documents, then this woman would be given a prison term for it, because all documents talking about persecution and pressure against believers was considered to be slander against "Soviet reality" (which is to say that the government effectively denied that any such persecution was going on).

This picture of Pavel Rumachik in 1975 would have been taken at about the time when these events transpired.

I said, "Here's what we'll do: I'll jump out the window, and if the coast is clear, then you pass the bag down to me so I can go run off and hide it." Everybody agreed, and it was a good thing that we lived on the first floor. I opened the window, looked to the right and the left, and saw no one. I jumped out, but no sooner had I jumped than people came out from behind the bushes and caught me before I even touched the ground.

"Why are you jumping out the window," they asked. "Don't you have a door?"

---

[87] The Ural Mountains: Formerly known as the *Kamennyi poyas* in Tsarist times, this is the mountain range used by geographers to denote the boundary between Europe and Asia. It is also the basic boundary between European Russia and Siberia, running more or less tangent to the 65th meridian. Someone form the Urals could arguably be considered to be from Siberia.

I said, "Sure we have a door, but there are a lot of people out in the hallway, making it so there's no way to get through that way."[88]

They began asking what I was doing, who was I and so on. I explained that I had jumped out the window so that I could explain to these people that our parents weren't home, and that I couldn't open the door to them.... They took me off to the police station, and I sat there for a while before they let me go. I came up to the front steps of the apartment building and waited

Pavel Rumachik standing by the window from which he jumped while attempting to save the literature from the KGB.

there until all the people left who were waiting outside the door. When they left, I was able to get back into the apartment. Eventually, the police left the area entirely, and we were able to save these documents.

The apartment building where the Rumachiks lived during those years that they were searched so often by the KGB.

When I was just about to turn 14, I began praying to God that He would give His blessing for me to get baptized. Summer came, and they began to hold lessons for those who wanted to get baptized. I began attending these classes, and the Lord blessed in this.

---

[88] In another account of this story, Brother Pavel added at this point that he had told them, "There are a lot of strangers out in the hall, and I was afraid to open the door because I didn't know who those people were."

Now, this was a very difficult time, a time when we were being fiercely persecuted. The authorities were not even allowing us to hold worship services, and we understood that they weren't going to let us have a baptism, either. There were a lot of people who wanted to get baptized—something on the order of 22 of us—so we decided to divide into two groups. One of these groups would get baptized Saturday late in the evening, and the other would get baptized early Sunday morning while the city was still asleep. We would hold baptisms at a reservoir, or lake, or perhaps some river out in the country.

So we passed the word along that we would meet in such-and-such a place, at such-and-such a house, and from there we would go to the baptism. We gathered there, and must have walked a full hour to the site of the baptism. This was so that we would be able to tell if anyone was following us, and we arrived at the lake quietly in stealth. I was supposed to be baptized in the evening on Saturday.

All the participants gathered at the river and were baptized. By the time we changed out of our wet clothes and finished the service, it was already dark, and under that cover we were able to return home unhindered and rejoicing. The next day, another group of people was baptized, thus sealing their covenant with the Lord. That Sunday we had a worship service in Nahabino on Krasnoarmeyskaya Street and took our first communion. There we gave our testimonies about how we came to the Lord. There were presents from the church and the ministers, and this was also when I was given the first Bible I ever owned. This was a beautiful time of fellowship, and what is even more amazing is that they didn't come to break up the services on that day.

Soon thereafter, however, they began to persecute us intensely in Nahabino, and we were unable to meet there anymore. The authorities exercised brutal means to pushed us out of that area. It is amazing, though, that we have such a miraculous and merciful God: now here it is right on twenty years later, and on that very same Krasnoarmeyskaya street, in the very same village of Nahabino, He has allowed us to buy a piece of land, and we are now building a church not far from the place where at one time they broke up our worship services in force. Now we are able to build here in peace, and we hope that by summer[89] we will be able to hold worship services there and that the perishing would be able to come to know the Lord.

It was, of course, a great problem for us that our father was never home. As I've already said, my father spent 18 and a half years in prison. Not only that, but even when he was not in prison it was not possible for him to live at home since he was part of an illegal organization. The authorities would keep a close eye on him whenever he would get out of prison, and he would have to check in with them to show them that everything was all right and that he was at home. Nonetheless, he had a ministry to carry out among the brotherhood, and this interfered with him being able to check in. He would miss checking in a couple of times, for which he was warned, and then they would begin preparing a case against him.

Whenever that would happen, my father would have to go into hiding. He would stay in the apartments of other believers, and we would not know where he was. We had very few opportunities to see our father during these times, but I especially remember the times God gave us to meet. This was when we would meet in the forest. You see, my father is very fond of hunting mushrooms. And as the summer waned, we knew that soon our father would send us a message through someone, saying, "Children, we will meet on such-and-such a day, at such-and-such a time, and ride the *elektrichka*[90] out of Moscow to go hunt mushrooms." This was a wonderful time, because not only could we see our father, but we could also go with him together into the forest to gather mushrooms, we could have lunch with him there in the forest, eating and rejoicing together. This was a very happy time for us children. We would gather mushrooms from the trees and all over the forest, and then as we were coming back, our father would hand us the bucket of mushrooms. At this point, our visit was over: we would part ways and bring the bucket back home. We were so very happy and thankful to God for these short visits that we were able to have!

---

[89] That is, by the summer of 1999.

[90] A type of electric commuter train common in the Soviet Union.

When our father was in prison, it was a great joy for us when we were able to go see him on visitation: to see his face and to talk with him. Sometimes, these were very short visits that might have lasted no more than an hour. These were what was called "common visitation," where there was a pane of glass separating us and we would talk to each other through telephone receivers. We couldn't even hug or kiss each other. This wasn't really as though we were meeting, but we could just sort of wave to each other from different sides of the glass.

Pavel Rumachik meeting in secret with his father in the woods in 1980. Because he was in exile at the time, Brother Peter had to be smuggled into Dedovsk to see his family.

There were other times when we were allowed personal visitation. This was once a year, when we were given a day or two—or at the maximum three— when the prisoner's wife and children could come see him. Of course, this was a long trip to make and was very expensive, so that mom would only take one of us at a time. We very much valued the opportunity to meet our father, and sometimes they would take even that away from us.

I remember one time when father was in Chita. My mother and I came to see him, and it was well below freezing. I didn't have a pair of good boots, so I asked my uncle to let me have his. He gave them to me, but they were tight on me and a bit too small. When we got off the train, we still had a way to travel on the *elektrichka*, and the *elektrichka* was so cold inside that there was snow on the floor inside that didn't melt. I did whatever I could to keep my feet warm by massaging them and so on, and praise God, we finally arrived at the stop where we were to get off. Even still, we had to take the bus from there into the zone, and I could feel that my feet were already frozen. It was 40 degrees below zero.[91] I was hoping that the bus

---

91 –40° C = –40° F

would have heat so that I could warm my feet, but as soon as we got on the bus, I saw with tears in my eyes that it was just the same as the *elektrichka*: here there was snow piled up on the floor just like before. We had to ride in that cold bus for a full hour, and then when we arrived, we still had to walk on foot to the camp. We were tired as we carried our heavy bags the rest of the way, but this was able to warm us up a little. When we finally arrived at the camp, we went in and told them that we had come for visitation rights. They replied, "Your father is not permitted to have visitation." As my mother began to ask why, they answered, "He has violated discipline." No matter how my mother tried to talk them out of this or to try to find some way to see him, they didn't budge. So we had to get back on these cold buses and transport and make our way back home, going all the long way back from Chita to Moscow (about 4,000 miles) and not having gotten the visit that we really should have gotten. Moreover, this happened on more than one occasion.

Even when my mother was able to have visitation rights, it was necessary to go through a very degrading inspection. We were searched from head to foot: they checked everything to make sure that we weren't bringing anything to father; all the foods that we brought him were cut up to make sure that we weren't smuggling anything in. Of course, this was all very degrading and unpleasant, but we understood that the joy of seeing our father was greater than all this.

Whenever we were in the room for visitation, we knew that they were spying on us, watching and listening. We knew that they had really sophisticated video cameras and listening devices, and when we wanted to discuss some important matter, we had to use gestures or some other method to make it so that they wouldn't be able to understand anything. Whatever the case, it was always a great joy for us that we could see our father and that he could see us. We always left these meetings happy and encouraged, even in these difficult times.

I remember one time when my father was sentenced to five years. This was during the Olympics in 1980 that were held in Moscow. In connection with this, there were a lot of security personnel in Moscow, many police, KGB, and other security forces; they occupied themselves with chasing down all the spies, drunks and other undesirables; after that, they sent all the convicts 100 kilometers outside of Moscow, so that Moscow would be a "civilized city." So in August of that year my father was arrested, sentenced to five years, and sent to Chita.

This was a very difficult period. We would write letters to our father, and they would not reach him; he would write us letters also, but they would not get to us either. Because he was under a strict disciplinary regime, our father only had the right to write no more than two letters a month. Even then, these letters would often not make it to us.

This was a tough five-year sentence, but it eventually came to an end. My mother and I began making plans to go meet my father. Mother had decided that I would be the one to go with her, since I had just finished my mandatory tour of duty in the army. Mom prepared a suit for my father to wear when he got out, and she mended it and checked the buttons; she added to this a nice shirt. This was a very important time for us, since the five years had ended, and now father was coming home to the family. Each of us children got ready as much as he was able. We got all the clothes and our food together for the trip, and were happy and rejoicing the while. As we left, everybody was eagerly awaiting our return.

We flew into Chita. We went to the market and my mother bought a bouquet of flowers. I remember that I also asked her for money, saying, "Mom, I want to buy some flowers to congratulate father on the occasion of his release." So I also bought a bouquet of white flowers. We were looking forward to that joyous meeting as we took all these flowers, food and clothes with us, and we went into the reception area of the prison compound. Mom went on into the receptionary, and I waited with the clothes, flowers and other things in the waiting room. My mother didn't come back for a long time. Then I looked up and saw her coming, and she had tears in her eyes. "Mama, what's happened?" I asked. "Is something not right?"

She answered me, "They're not going to release your father."

"What do you mean they're not going to release him," I asked.

"He is not here," she said. "They have taken him into the city, where they are holding him in isolation for investigation, and they've said that they will be bringing another criminal case against him. He is not here. Some problems have come up."

We went into the city, and there they told us, "Yes, three days ago they sent your father here from the camp, and there is a criminal case being opened against him. They want to extend his sentence."

Mom began asking why, since he was a good man, honest and forthright. They answered, "We don't know anything about that. That is not our affair." Then we understood that they really weren't going to let father go. Of course, this was news that we weren't expecting, and we weren't really sure what to do. Then we decided to leave these flowers in the waiting room where people came to pick up their relatives, and also for the woman that had given us this information.

We went home. Of course, when we arrived, everybody was waiting for us, and here we had come home without father. This was certainly very hard for us to understand and reconcile in our minds, but it was the reality: they were not going to release our father. He was tried again, and a term of five years was added on to his sentence because he had not mended his ways and because he remained faithful to the Lord.

■ ■ ■ ■ ■

So, WHAT IS MY OVERALL opinion of my father, and what role did he play in my life? I am very thankful to God that my father was a minister of the Lord throughout the entire course of his life, and no matter how long he was in prisons and concentration camps, he was always serving the Lord. His was a great and a good example. I understand clearly that he was a genuine Christian both in his ministry and in his suffering for God.

There was a Christian summer camp that was held especially for the children of fathers who were either in prison for the faith or who were on the lam, and I remember the counselors asking us there, "Children, what would you like to be when you grow up?" It was always clear that I should be a minister, so the question was more specific, meaning, what kind of minister did I want to be? Someone said, "I want to be a pastor." Someone else said, "A preacher." Still others said that they wanted to be deacons or choir directors. And I always answered, "I want to be an evangelist." It was the good example of my father that inspired this desire in me. I am thankful to God that He has given me the opportunity to labor for Him and serve His holy name. The faithfulness of my father strengthened me to that end, and I thank the Lord and my father for this wonderful example that I had from my earliest childhood.

THE TESTIMONY OF
LUBA RUMACHIK

DEAR BROTHERS AND SISTERS, I greet you all in the love of our Lord Jesus Christ, and I want to share briefly with you the story of my life.

Luba Rumachik and her two young children in 1961 posing with Luba's mother, 5 brothers and one sister. The life of Luba's mother served as a godly example to her daughter, since Mrs. Smirnov was also called upon to raise many children on her own during the four times that Luba's father was imprisoned for the faith.

I was born on March 25, 1936. I was raised in a Christian family, and my parents told me from the earliest age about God's love. They prayed for me, that God would protect me in this world; and not only me, but also all my brothers and sisters. My parents had seven children, and we all love the Lord to this day.

In 1955, the Lord sent me my life's companion, Peter Rumachik. We lived with my parents in a room in their private home. This was the home were we also held worship services.

After the death of Stalin, the persecutions stopped in our country, but in 1961, they began anew to persecute the faithful. They tried my husband, my father, and my two uncles for their faith in God. They were sentenced as *parasites*, meaning that they were tried for not working, even though they all had jobs that they worked. These men were sent off to remote Siberia, and I was left at home with two small children.

Peter Rumachik and Luba Smirnova in 1955.

Luba Rumachik as a young mother with her first two children in 1961.

So it was that in 1961 we experienced the first major trial in our lives. They searched our house. Three months after the search, our two-year-old daughter died. Three months after that, they arrested my husband, and three months later I learned that he had broken his leg there. At the time, I was working in the factory where I had worked since I was sixteen. When I found out he was in the hospital, I asked permission at my job for them to release me to go to my husband, and they allowed me to go to my husband so that I could spend this time with him in exile. My relatives tried to talk me out of it, saying, "Where do you think you're going, off to distant Siberia? You don't know anyone there or anything about that place!"

"The Lord is my Help," I said. "He will never forsake me." When my relatives saw my firmness and that I was definitely going to go, they sent the children of their brother and cousin with me as well so that I would take them to their fathers.

And so in February 1962, I was 25 years old when I set off with five children bound for distant Siberia. We travelled by train for three days, and then had to switch to travelling by plane. The road was very difficult. There were so many planes

Luba Rumachik with a friend at the train station as she departs for Siberia in 1962.

backed up that it was impossible to take off. I walked up to the cashier at the ticket window and said to her, "Please help me get a flight out of here. I have five little children with me."

She answered, "I can't. People have already been waiting here for weeks."

I said, "Young lady, please help us." Then I set my things down in front of the cashier's window and had the five little children sit down. Then I sat down with them.

I looked up to see the cashier beckoning to me with her finger. She said to me, "Your flight will be leaving shortly."

When we arrived at the next airport, it was the same situation. There were so many flights backlogged that it was impossible to leave. Again I went up to the cashier and asked her to help me get a flight out for myself and the five small children that were with me. She was amazed that I had so many children, and here I was so young. We all sat down again just like before in front of the cashier's window, so that she could see us, and all the while I was praying to the Lord that He would work in the heart of this woman so that she would sympathize for our plight. She called me after a brief while and said, "Your flight will be leaving shortly."

I had already sent my things on ahead to my father—who lived further on than my husband—because I knew that my husband was in the hospital (though, in actuality, he had already been released). Since my father knew I was coming, he was supposed to meet me at the airport. The plane they had put us on, however, was an unusual one: they had gotten us out on a freight plane, so that the children and I were the only ones on the flight and nobody was expected to get on or off of it. (This meant that my father would not know how to find us when we arrived.)

And so we arrived finally at Balturino, which was the name of the airport. This was a small facility out in the middle of nowhere, with wooden benches and everything else one would expect to find in "the sticks." I went up to the cashier and asked, "Miss, could you please tell me how to get to the village of Prosikhina?"

She answered, "There's no way for you to get there. This is the weekend, and there is no transportation running out that way today."

I went and laid my things out on the bench and lay down with the children. As we lay down, I was thinking that the children and I would spend the night here and perhaps be able to leave the next morning. I prayed about this all to the Lord as I lay down, and it wasn't long before He came to my aid: in just a few moments, the woman called to me and said, "Ma'am hurry quick! The ambulance is getting ready to leave for the village! They'll take you there!"

We gathered our things, got into the ambulance, and took off. We had hardly gotten to the village before we were forced to stop because of a large crowd of people standing in the road. It turned out that this was a funeral procession, and that, along with all the snow, made it impossible to get through, since the roads were narrow. No sooner had the ambulance stopped and the doors opened, but here my dad came walking up. How amazing! My father didn't even have the slightest idea that I would be taking a mail plane in, or that I be coming in such an unusual fashion to the village, but here he just happened to be walking past when I arrived! We were then able to go on by car together to where my husband was.

Peter and Luba Rumachik in Siberia, 1963.

At this time, the weather was very severe: the temperature was hovering at 50 below (and even lower).[92]

And so I came to my husband, and our meeting was a very joyous occasion. After dinner, we were sitting at the table, and he asked me, "Will you be staying long?"

And I answered, "I'll be staying for always."

"What do you mean, 'For always'?" he said.

"Just that."

"Don't you have a job where you have to be?" he asked.

---

[92] –50° C = –59° F

"I quit so that I could come here to be with you, so that we could bring praise to the Lord together and share these hard times that the Lord has allowed us to endure," I said.

We were given a dormitory room to live in, and we held meetings there—my husband speaks more about this in his account. We lived there for four years, after which we returned to Dyedovsk. We had four children at this time, since two more were born to us while we were in exile: Nadya and Pavlusha,[93] the latter of which is now laboring as a missionary.

■ ■ ■ ■ ■

WHEN I CAME TO KRASNOGORSK to give birth to our son—who ended up weighing 5 kg, 100 g[94]—this was a terrible time for me, because the midwife knew I was a Baptist. I could clearly sense that she wanted me to die, and she did everything she could to try to kill me. At that time, the director of the maternity ward came in and asked how I was feeling. I proceeded to tell her the whole story, and she immediately had me put on an I.V. through which I was able to re-gain my strength.

After the exile, the persecutions began again, and they began to keep watch on the brethren, and among them my husband. Another daughter, Valya,[95] was born to us at this time. I remember how, when my husband came and brought her home from the maternity ward, we prayed over her and thanked the Lord for her, for she was our fifth child. Then my husband turned to me and said, "I have to go. I must be about the Lord's work, and I cannot stay here any longer. I must leave now."

I said to him, "Go." We prayed again, and with that, he left.

I was left at home now with five children.

Not long after this, the authorities showed up from Voronezh to search our home. My husband had been taken into custody, but the operatives

---

93 *Pavlusha:* that is, "Paulie." A diminutive form of "Pavel"

94 Approx. 11 lbs., 4 oz.

95 *Valya:* A diminutive form of Valentina

didn't tell me that he had been arrested. Instead, they asked me, "Lubov Vasilievna, where is your husband?"

After the search was concluded, I got to thinking: "Why did they come all the way from Voronezh? Maybe they've arrested Pete...." So I took up our six-month old daughter Valya and put her in a sling against my shoulders; then I took a package[96] and slung it over my back. Then I went off to look for my husband.

When I got to Voronezh, I didn't stop to ask anybody where my husband was, but went directly to the prison. I knew that if they accepted the package there for my husband, that would mean that they had him in custody. When I gave them the package, they received it, and I gave thanks to the Lord that I had found my husband.

Luba Rumachik and her mother pose with Luba's children in 1976. Notably, Peter Rumachik is missing from this picture since he was in prison at the time.

Later, they transferred him from Voronezh to Moscow. I took my five children and went to see him for visitation. We were given visitation rights for two hours, where we had to talk to each other from opposite sides of a pane of glass. Next to us the whole time, a guard sat keeping tabs on our conversation. When we went into this room, my husband looked at our five small children, and tears appeared in his eyes. Pavlushka kept his head down on the table, for he couldn't even look at his father's face, and he cried for the whole duration of the visit. I saw the tears forming in Pete's eyes, and I began praying, "Dear Lord, just please help me not to cry, so that my husband would never see my tears and detect the woe behind them. Help me to be cheerful, so that it will

---

[96] In this sense, a package of foodstuffs and other items to be given to a prisoner.

be easier for him to bear all these trials." And the Lord gave me strength, so that when I saw the tears in his eyes, I said, "Pete, what is there to cry about? We have no reason to cry. Today we get to see each other, and we are alive and well."

Of course, these were not just simple tears that he had, but they were also tears of concern, because not only was he alone there, but we were alone here on the other side as well without our father. And now these children would have to be brought up without their father in this time of difficulties, this time of trials and persecution for being faithful to the Lord.

It was very difficult to raise the children. Ours was an atheist country. My children were pressured at school from the beginning to don the Octobrists' pin, but my children were never Octobrists, nor Pioneers, nor Komsols. The Lord helped me to watch after them. I took concern over their souls, and exerted all my strength to watch out for them. I received help from the Lord to do this just as I had requested it. The Lord helped me in all this, and now that my children are grown, they are seeking the Lord's face and keeping the faith of their parents.

It was also hard on the children for them to grow up without their father, just as it was hard for me to raise them without a husband. The persecutions intensified in our country. Some of our brethren who went off to serve in the army were put in prison because they remained faithful, and because they didn't yield and take up arms. Some were beaten. But the Word gives us hope that the Lord can save those who are condemned to death.[97] And along with them, I decided to bear this difficult labor and serve the Lord by working on the Women's committee for the defense of those persecuted for their faithfulness to the Lord.

I was heavily persecuted because of my work on this committee. I was constantly being watched. There were constant threats. We were constantly being "bugged": everything was listened in on or spied on in our apartment. We couldn't even speak freely in our own home. Sometimes I would have to go to Moscow to send as many as forty telegrams at one time petitioning

---

[97] The author's choice of words indicates that she is referring to Psalm 79:11, which reads, "Let the sighing of the prisoner come before thee; according to the greatness of thy power preserve thou those that are appointed to die…"

Luba Rumachik (far right, first row) with the "Women's Council of Prisoners' Relatives" on which she served from 1967–1987.

the government, and I wouldn't be able to say openly where I was going. I could only signal with my hands that I was going to send off telegrams, and that if I didn't return then it meant I had been put in prison. I couldn't say this out loud, but the children understood me. Prayerfully, I left. I went to Moscow to send off telegrams. Every step of the way I was ready for someone to walk up to me, take me by the arm, and say, "Luba, let's go: you're under arrest." You had to have a lot of strength to do this, but that strength was only in God. So I would get down on my knees and pray that the Lord would give me the strength to endure all of this.

The operatives of the KGB knew of our work and that we were trying to publicize the knowledge of what was going on in our country. We knew that they wanted to subdue us, but this was impossible, for the Lord was with us. We all had a lot of children: one woman had 10, another 8, yet another had 6…So it would have been a hard thing for them to throw us all in jail. But there were still women on this committee like Lydia Mikhailovna Vins, who served three years of prison time for her work. We continued this work, however, and we were fully prepared to go to prison for our faithfulness to God.

Once the authorities called me in and told me: "If you take your children to church services again, we'll take your kids away and throw you in jail." When I came home, my eldest daughter asked me, "Mama, what did they say to you?" I told her what they had said. She asked, "So mama, are you going to keep going to the services?" And I said, "Without a doubt. And I'm taking all of you with me. The Lord will protect us."

It was so hard for the children to live through all this. Every day we prayed to the Lord that He would keep us all faithful, that He would be with papa in prison, that He would support me in this difficult labor and these threats to remain confident. At this time, they were already taking children away from their parents, and our children knew this. It was hard for them, but I encouraged the children: "Surrender yourselves to the Lord. Even if the Lord were to allow me to be arrested, and you would be left without a mother or a father, then you have a Heavenly Father—your very best Friend—Who will never leave you. If they take you away, then remember that there will come a time when, through your prayers and ours, that the Lord will return you once again to your parents.

There were times when I would have to leave the children to be looked after by their oldest sister (who was 14 or 15 at the time) for three and four days at a time. I would prepare their food in advance and put it in the fridge for them. My daughter had to go to school, as did the other children who were very small. I couldn't invite any of my sisters to come sit with the kids, because none of them could understand why I was doing this: "Where did I think I was going," they would ask, "after there had already been so many threats made?" Therefore, I prayed to the Lord that He would protect my children in my absence. And the Lord protected them.

Once while I was away, we weren't able to get everything done in the time we had alotted for ourselves, so I had to stay another day. Everybody was asking, "Luba, where are your kids?" I replied, "With the Lord. They're with the Lord. Let's pray." So the other women and I prayed. The others on the committee all lived with their parents, but my children and I lived alone. I tried not to tell my parents how I had to leave the children alone at times, because I didn't want them to worry.

The persecutions were fierce. My father also served time for the Lord, and there was a period of 30 years when my father and my husband didn't see each other. The authorities would arrest my husband while my father was in prison, so that when he would get out, my husband would be behind bars. Then my husband would get out only to find that my father had been arrested again. It went on this way as a seemingly endless cycle. The KGB worked in such a way as to see to it that we weren't even able to see each other. But even in this may the Lord be praised.

I was concerned that I had had to stay an extra day to get all this work done. I came home, and Pavel came up to me with tears in his eyes: "Vera fed us such awful stuff that it was just scary!"

I said, "Son, are you all still alive?"

"Yes, we're alive."

"Then, praise God!"

In this way, the Lord protected my children. No matter what threats we faced, the Lord shielded us. The Lord did not allow me to be put in prison. The Lord did not allow my children to be taken away. He gave us the strength and the increase to carry on. I thank the Lord for all these things.

Our worship services were held in my parents' house. In 1961 when my father, husband and uncle were arrested, it was the decision of the court to confiscate the house, partition it, and rent out part of it to us: the original occupants. My parents were given two rooms, and in one of the rooms I lived with my newborn infant. For two months, I kept the child on the table. Of course, a baby should never be kept on a table, but there was nowhere else to put her.

I put all the children's beds together, but I still had to put her bed by the window. She got sick often. I wrote a letter of appeal to the city authorities, explaining how my living quarters had been confiscated so that I now had nowhere to live. In effect, I asked in the letter that I be given a place to live. The government was opposed to this, but the Lord had His own intentions.

Eventually, the authorities gave me a new three-room apartment in which to live. When the KGB found out about it, they hit the roof and demanded, "No, we will not allow this woman to live in a new building. She has to have a poor house with no electricity or gas." So I wasn't registered to live in that house. My husband was in prison at the time, and his term was close to expiring. I continued living there without registration for six months. I wrote the Moscow Prosecutor's Office, explaining that I was being threatened with a fine for not being registered. I asked, "Who should be fined: me, or those who refuse to register me?" I had already been renting the apartment for 6 months, and I paid the rent each month on time, so the decision was made to register me.

My husband was released soon after that, but we couldn't just have a nice, quiet life. The persecutions in our country continued, and it wasn't long before my husband was being investigated again. Again, he went to continue his work underground, and soon after that he was arrested. He was sent very far away, and while he was gone our son Gyena[98] was born. I received a letter from him in which he wrote, "Luba, I've been permitted to have personal visitation." This meant that we would be able to be together in the same room, that we would be able to talk together, to cook and eat together. "But I cannot ask you to come," he continued, "because I know that you have little Gyena there." Gyena was two months old at the time. I was so overjoyed at the possibility of seeing my husband, however, that I decided to go anyway. One of the elder brothers in the church helped me with my luggage as I flew there, and I carried this little baby in my arms. When I arrived, the whole camp was in a hubbub about how I had travelled so many long kilometers from far-away Moscow with such a small baby to see my husband. People were even more amazed as some of them commented, "Our wives live close by and don't come to see us, yet here this woman comes to see her husband from far-off Moscow with a newborn."

I came to the office of the commandant to announce my arrival as required. As I stood in line waiting for admittance, I saw many of the officers going into the commandant's office. For some reason, this put me ill at ease, and I very nearly got the shakes as I felt that something was not right here. I thought that all these people going in there had something to do with keeping me from seeing my husband. I began praying that the Lord would give me the wisdom to tell them of Christ and about how He loves them.

As I went into the commandant's office, the first question they asked me was, "Is your husband a believer?"

I answered, "Yes, but not only is my husband a believer: I am a believer, too. As I was flying here, I was just amazed at how the Lord had so miraculously ordered everything...."

---

[98] *Genya:* A diminutive form of Yevgeny

I began to tell them of Christ. The listened for a long time, then one of the officers said, "You know, your husband is such a terrible cultist.[99] He is a threat to the establishment."

The commandant replied, "That has nothing to do with us. Our business is to see that he serves out his term. But you know, we only give visitation rights to those prisoners that work well. Your husband hasn't made a good showing of himself."

I replied, "He hasn't had the chance yet to make a good showing; he's only been in this camp for two months. Once he gets the chance to work some more, you'll see what a wonderful husband I have."

Then the brigade commander said to the commandant, "As you know, sir, I am the commander of his platoon. This is such a good person, that I have never met anyone like this before. He works superbly."

"Then why didn't you say anything?!" the commandant asked. "Why isn't that written in his work evaluation log?"

The other replied, "We don't have the right to put down anything in that log until the prisoner has been in camp for three months. If he had been here for three months, then I would have written only good things about him."

Then the commandant asked me, "Tell me, did you pray to God while you were on your way here for visitation?"

I answered, "Yes, but not only did I pray: our whole church prayed that the Lord would open your hearts to doing a good thing for us here."

The commandant hung his head low and didn't speak for some time. I was thinking that he might retort with something like, "Well then, you have your God to help you, and I won't give you visitation rights. So go on back home with your baby." But then he raised his head and said, "Yes… God heard your prayer, and I'm giving you three days of visitation without work call." This meant that I was going to be able to be with my husband for three full days and nights and he wouldn't have to go out to work. Other wives when they came to see their husbands would only get to see them in the evenings, since the men would be required to go out to work during the day. This way, however, we had three full days to be together: my husband, myself, and our newborn child. Again, the Lord helped us in

---

[99] Baptists in the Soviet Union were portrayed as the members of a religious cult.

all things. Praise Him for this! What a joyful time that was for my husband to be with his young son and wife. In all these trials and tribulations, the Lord sent us joy. Praise Him for that!

We were only allowed to have these sorts of visiting rights once a year. That was during the fall of 1970. As the fall of 1971 was now upon us and it was time for visiting rights again, my husband wrote me to say, "Luba, we won't be having any visitation rights this time because the prison is under quarantine." How I had looked forward to this visit, and now we were not going to have it.

In February of 1972, our 16-year-old daughter died. This was due to an error on the part of the doctors. For two years, she had high blood pressure, then she developed a fever. The doctors said that this was nothing more than a flu, but it turned out that she actually had kidney failure. These were hard trials to face when I came to the medical institute and the doctors told me that they wanted to do a kidney transplant. This was hard, because my husband was not around, neither was there any close relative who could help me make this decision. So before the Lord I decided to go ahead with the transplant. I didn't know why all these things had happened this way, and only later did it become clear.

I prayed that, if it was the Lord's will, that He would heal her without this operation. But if it was His will for her to die, that He would allow her to die without her having to be cut by a surgeon's knife.

Once I came to the institute where my daughter was being kept. The doctor came up to me and said, "Your daughter…will not live until the operation." Her hemoglobin count was at 32 with nitrogen levels at 290. When the doctor said this, it was as if he had plunged a dagger into my heart, but I thanked God: He had answered my prayer that she would not have a knife lifted to her if she were to die.

I did not dare to ask the Lord to leave her alive as my aunt had done. When her son was dying, my aunt cried out to the Lord in prayer, "Lord, spare him! Lord, spare him!" And the Lord spared him. For many years after that she was tormented by his life, then she died. He remains a drunk to this very day.

Therefore, I prayed, "Lord, Thy will be done." Our daughter loved the Lord very much. She played the piano and the accordian. She sang and praised the Lord. At church, everybody loved her. I knew that if she died, she would be with the Lord.

The professor said, "Go ahead and visit your daughter so long as you don't ask her any questions. Just talk about whatever she wants."

I went in to her room, and my heart sank when I saw the state she was in. She said, "Mama, I'm so glad to see you! You haven't come to see me in such a long time!"

I asked, "How's your health, dear...?"[100] The doctor immediately cut me short.

My daughter replied, "Good, mama. Nothing hurts at all."

I understood immediately that the reason why nothing hurt was because her kidney failure had poisoned her to the point that she couldn't feel anything anymore.

I said, "Dear, what would you like to eat?"[101]

At this, the professor said, "Alright, the visit is over. Let's go."

I came home, and we decided to take her out of the hospital so that we could use herbal medicine to heal her at home, but it was already too late.

I came with my sister Lucy to bring her home, but the professor refused to let us take her, saying, "You can't take her out of here. She's in such bad shape that she'll die before you get her home."

I replied, "I don't know who's going to die first: me, or my daughter, but I want to take her home."

He decided to let me observe her condition for myself, and when I walked into her room, she was already on a respirator. I asked, "Daughter, would you like to go home?"

She replied, "Oh yes, mama, I want to go home very much."

"Daughter, I'm going to take you home," I said, and left the room so that she wouldn't see my tears. To the doctor I said, "I'm taking her home. I want you to discharge her from the ward."

They let her out that very day, and she came home still on oxygen. When we arrived, we prayed for her, and during the prayer I became ill at heart. They took me into the next room. There I sat dying, as my daughter

---

[100] In this case, inquiring about one's health is a Russian greeting.

[101] In Russian hospitals, the family—rather than the institution—prepares the food for the patients.

was dying in the next room. I prayed, "Lord, I have many small children left. (Vovik had just been born.) Please just keep me alive for the sake of these little ones who are left. Nevertheless, let Your will be done." I lay there on the bed in a swoon. The window was open even though it was February. When my daughter died, however, the weight was lifted. There were others with her in the room when she passed away at 11:05 at night. It was a long time before they were able to tell me that she had died, but I already knew, for I could feel it in my heart. My brother finally got up the courage to tell me, and I responded, "Praise God. The Lord giveth, and the Lord taketh away."

I felt awful, and was still lying on the bed when they called my father away to have a word with him. They told him, "Be careful that the same thing doesn't happen here that happened in Radiska. In that town the child of some believers had drowned, and the townspeople snatched the coffin away from the pallbearers and threw rocks at them. We began to pray fervently.

When we left the apartment, the entranceway was so packed with an angry mob that it was quite nearly impossible to get through. All around us, the place was just packed with people. I prayed, "Lord, protect us."[102]

As the relatives carried the coffin on their shoulders, several of these people came up to my father, saying, "Come, let us help you carry the coffin." My father replied, however, that he would rather just carry it on his own shoulders. In this way the Lord protected us. I praise the Lord for this.

At this time, there were fierce persecutions against Christians: they broadcast on the radio, by television, and in film that we [the Baptists] offered up our children in human sacrifice. Our entire city was filled with the rumor that I had sacrificed my daughter. After her funeral whenever I would go to work or the store, people would point their finger right at me and say, "That woman right there killed her daughter in human sacrifice."

---

[102] As the author goes on to say, the Soviet government carried out an active campaign of slander against the Baptists. In this case, the very Soviet system whose doctors were responsible by their neglect for the death of this girl was the same Soviet system that spread the outright lie that the Rumachiks had offered their daughter in human sacrifice to God; the result was that an angry mob was incited, and the authorities had to step in to prevent the violence from getting out of hand.

It was very hard to endure all this, but praise the Lord that through these difficulties we were able to remain faithful to Him. After our daughter's death, my husband sent me a letter, saying, "Luba, they have allowed me to have personal visitation rights." I went to him. Praise God that we had this visit not in the fall as it should have been, but in February right after my daughter's death. How miraculously God had worked all this out. We were only given visitation rights once a year, and who else could have been a comfort to my husband at this time. Only we could understand each other in our tribulation. After this terrible loss of our daughter, in tears we could comfort one another with the knowledge that the Lord would help us. We thanked the Lord so much that He cared for us and that in these tribulations and difficult times He gave us the chance to meet even here in this prison.

1972 funeral for 16-year-old daughter who died of kidney failure. Though the events surrounding her death clearly put the Soviet doctors at fault for malpractice, it was widely rumored that she had been offered in human sacrifice.

Our worship services were constantly being broken up. Threats were regularly being made against me. KGB operatives were continually yelling at me, "Luba Rumachik, we'll throw you in jail and take away your kids!"

The church at that time knew very little about our labor on the women's committee because this was a very tough time and we tried to keep our activities under wraps. Finally, however, we decided to bring this all out in the open. I remember that a journal was published in which there was a petition on behalf of our persecuted brothers and sisters in our land, and there was my signature under it, the second from the top. My dad saw that my signature was there, and he was gravely concerned, because this journal was distributed throughout the entire Soviet Union, and now the authorities would know for sure that I was involved in this sort of ministry.

A criminal case began to be built against me. Operatives from the prosecutor's office came to the school and asked what my kids were like. We had 7 children in school, and my husband and I had 8 children total. The teachers really loved my children, and they were so well behaved that they just shone. The teachers answered, "The children are lovely; there's nothing at all bad that can be said about them. Their mother has brought them up very well."

The operatives went to the hospital, and there they asked how I got on with the doctors and how I treated my children. They also said, "Very well. This mother really looks out for her children. Any time any one of them gets sick, she immediately notifies us: 'Come quickly, my child has fallen ill'."

They couldn't find anything to incriminate me, neither from the teachers nor the doctors. Nevertheless, the operatives of the KGB were set very much against me because I brought my children up in a Christian spirit and from their earliest childhood and taught them to have faith in God.[103] It was very difficult during this time of persecution—very difficult—but I asked God for the strength to put my children on His path.

Once, one of the teachers came to me and said, "Lubov Vasilevna, why did your daughter die? They offered to take her in at the institute to do an operation on her, and you refused."

I replied, "That's not true. I didn't refuse. I put her in the hospital and agreed to the operation, but they didn't do the operation in time." I showed her the documentation from the hospital proving this. She agreed that it was so.

Then she said, "You know, everyone is saying that you sacrificed her."

"Let them say it," I replied. "False rumours have always been spread about Christians."

She said, "Tomorrow we're inducting all the kids into the Octobrists, and Valya will be inducted with them."

"I'll keep her home from school, then."

"That's great!" she answered. "I'm so glad you decided to do it that way."

---

[103] Or, "…*belief* in God." The Russian original here allows for either translation.

So the next day, all the kids were inducted into the Octobrists. When they asked, "Where's Valya Rumachik?" the teacher replied, "She's at home sick." This teacher really loved Valya, and in this fashion the Lord protected her. Praise the Lord for that!

In our country, the persecution against [Christian] children was very fierce. Some children got beat up at school. Others were taken away, while their parents where stripped of their paternal rights and put in prison. The same was true in our family, when our oldest son Misha went off to serve in the army and they wanted to have him court-martialed. Nonetheless, the Lord sent His protection for him. They also wanted to try our son Pavel: there were several believers there where he was serving, and they gathered together for prayer and reading the Word of God; Pavel was sort of the leader of this group. In their midst was a traitor who turned them in to the commandant's office. They found the literature that they had there, and they also wanted to try him for the fact that they gathered for prayer and read the Bible.

I came to visit Pavel while he was there, and he told me about all this. So we decided that, if I stopped getting mail from Pavel, it would mean that they had put in him in prison pending trial. Every day, I waited for a letter from Pavel, but there was none. I decided that this must mean they had arrested him. At this time, my husband was in prison. I decided to go to my son and give him a parcel of the kind that he would get in prison. As I put things into the box for my son, I sang,

> Now I am bearing a parcel
> To my dear son…

There were tears in my eyes, and my heart was heavy albeit not crushed. I accepted everything as being from the hands of God, and I believed in the wisdom of God's hand. I entrusted my children into God's hand. I prayed to the Lord that He would give them the strength to be faithful to Him and that they would be just like their dad.

I came to the military compound and walked up to the young soldier there who was on watch. I said, "Son, go call Pavel Rumachik for me, please." My heart was already sinking in anticipation as I expected him to say, "He's not here."

But instead he replied, "I'll go fetch him right away." I just couldn't understand it: I was thinking, "Can it be that this young man doesn't know my son is in prison?"

I stood there waiting, and, as I watched, I saw my Pavlik coming toward me: thin, pale, tall. We embraced.

He said, "Mama, what are you doing here?"

I answered, "Son, I've come to bring you a parcel."

I went to the commandant's office to get cleared for visitation rights, and, to make a long story short, we came into a room for visitation.

He said to me, "Mama, what kind of goodies did you bring?"

I answered, "Son, I don't have any goodies at all. I brought you the standard 5 kilo parcel: this is ham, sugar, warm socks…all the essentials for prison."

So we sat there and talked and prayed together. It turns out that, no sooner did we part company after my first visit, but Pavel fell ill with a kidney problem and they put him in the hospital. That's why he was totally unable to write me any letters. Since he had just gotten out of the hospital, and the time of his release from the service was already approaching, I put in a request with headquarters that they let him return with me. They replied, "No, we won't allow that. We send people [home] on our own trains and give them our own food…."

I said, "You know well that he was just released from the hospital. Just take a look for yourself how he looks. Therefore, I implore you: let him come with me. I'll give him completely different food, not the kind that you'll be feeding him."

And you know, the Lord came to my aid so that we went home together. The road was difficult, however. Everything was listened in on and watched. They had also told him that if anything happened when he came to Dyedovsk or if they caught him in any worship service or meeting there, then the case would be reopened on the basis of that evidence and he would be tried under those prior pretexts. But praise the Lord, he was not tried! The lord is greater than all these things, and to this day Pavel has remained free and is now a missionary serving the Lord. Thanks be to the Lord in all things!

Our family endured over 15 searches.[104] This was so hard, to watch as before our very eyes they would take away our literature. One time, the police and the operatives of the KGB came to search our home, and my husband was there. I understood that they were going to arrest him. As they searched the house, I sat at the sewing machine, sewed a bag for him, and put in it all the necessities for prison.

Once the search was over, the operatives and the police said to my husband, "Peter Vasilievich, come with us. We won't keep you long, but just for a short while."

He answered, "I know all about these 'short whiles'. I've seen 'short whiles' last for three years sometimes. Please let me go into the room here and pray with my loved ones."

We went into the room there, where the children were sleeping after their lunch. We got down on our knees and prayed. All the while these men were banging at the door, telling us that we were taking too long. He kissed the children and left the room, saying, "I won't go on my own. God's Word says, 'They shall bring you.'[105] So they took him as I handed the bag to him. And he didn't come back: they put him in prison for three years after that. It was very difficult, of course, in prison; my husband talks about that in his part of this book. Not only did they take away our being together, but they took away visitation rights, they took away parcels, and they took our correspondence.

Once, my daughter Nadya and I went for visitation. We flew 9 hours by plane. After that, we had to travel from there by train, and that evening as we were travelling the Lord revealed to me that they weren't going to give

---

[104] In his account, Pavel recalls "over 15 searches." Mrs. Rumachik seems to recall that the number may have been closer to 18 total searches.

[105] Matthew 10:18 "*And ye shall be brought* before governors and kings for my sake, for a testimony against them and the Gentiles." The Russian Synodal Version reads, "And they shall bring you…," since in Russian the active third-person plural is often used to denote what in English is rendered in passive voice. Another possible way of reading this passage in Russian is, "And they shall compel you…."

us visitation rights. I said, "Daughter, they're not going to give us visitation rights. God has told this to me in my sleep to prepare us for it.

When we arrived at the prison, two officers came up to meet us. We greeted them, and they replied, "What are you doing here?"

We answered, "We have come for visitation."

"You won't be getting any visitation."

"Why not?" we asked.

"He's been denied visitation rights."

Of course, it was very hard to accept all this, but as Christians we were ready for whatever the Lord allowed in our lives. This sort of visit was given only once a year, and now they had taken even that from us.

When we talk about these visits, it's hard to paint an accurate picture of what that was like, how they checked everything over with such exactitude. They would undress us to our undergarments, and often they would even remove those. They looked over every article of clothing and went through everything. All the foods were cut up with a knife. They poked forks through everything. Once when I came to visit, I had my broken arm in a cast. They unwound the cast and even checked that. They were so afraid that I might sneak in some sort of note for my husband. They stooped to such levels that it's unpleasant to talk about it, how before letting us in for visitation they would strip us down to nothing and have us sit there. These were the kind of things we wives had to endure along with our husbands.

During the visits, we couldn't talk about any serious matters, since everything was listened in on and watched. We weren't allowed to have pencil or paper so that we wouldn't pass any notes between ourselves. But the Lord gave us such wisdom that we only had to say two words to each other, and we already knew the entire thought. So nevertheless we were still able to tell each other everything.

■ ■ ■ ■ ■

FOR HIS FIFTH PRISON TERM, they gave my husband five years' incarceration. During one of our visits, he told me that it was very hard for him, and he could feel that the enemy wanted to eliminate him while he was there. "If there are no letters from me, it will mean that they've put me in isolation," he told me. "I won't take any food if they put me in there, but I will turn to the Lord in fasting and prayer and say to Him, 'May Your will be done.' He has the power to release me from isolation, but if His name would be glorified by my death, then I am ready to die." Our visit was drawing to a close, and as we sat there on the bed we decided to sing, "What Awaits Me, I Know Not."[106] This was a song that contained our entire life story inside it. We began to sing together. Then he started crying as I continued singing. Then he picked it up and sang as I cried. In that way, we got through the whole song, and it was in that painful way that we separated. We could feel in our hearts [that this might be the end], but we prayed to the Lord that He would help us to bear all things and to remain faithful to Him.

A little time passed, and I received a letter from a prisoner that told me, "Your husband is in isolation. He's not taking any food, and he is going to die there because they've given him 60 days." I immediately flew to where my husband was. He was very far away: over 5,000 kilometers.[107] Our enemies always tried to hide him from us.

Since I bore the responsibility of a ministry in which I could get out a telegram to say that my husband was in isolation and not receiving food, that they were trying to have him eliminated, I had to go to the prison myself. If the accusations turned out to be false, then I could be given a prison term for slander against the Soviet government. So I went with a parcel, since the time had come when he was allowed to receive one. As I walked up to the fence, I was met by a prisoner who told me, "Your husband is in isolation and is not taking any food." I couldn't trust that source either, however, since this could have been a specially designed entrapment. I came up to the controller and said, "I have brought my husband a parcel. The regulations allow it at this time."

"No, it's not allowed," he answered.

"Why not?" I asked.

"He is in isolation."

"What for?"

"For violation of discipline."

---

[106] The words to this song are contained in the appendix.

[107] 3,000 miles.

I rejoiced greatly that I was able to hear this straight from his mouth. Now I could take some sort of steps to lighten my husband's situation. I went to the commandant and asked, "Tell me, please: where is my husband?"

He said, "Here."

"Why has it been so long now that I haven't gotten any letters from him?" I inquired.

"Everything's fine with him," he replied.

"I happen to know that he's in solitary confinement."

"No."

"What do you mean, 'No'?"

"Who told you he's in solitary confinement?"

"The controller told me," I answered.

"Ah, yes, yes…."

I said, "Is he taking food?"

He said, "He's taking food, everything is as it should be."

"I know that he's not taking food," I answered.

"Who told you?" he asked.

"My husband told me. He told me that if you put him in the hole then he wouldn't take any food." I said, "For what violation was my husband put in isolation?"

The commandant answered, "He was put in because he wrote his sister a letter."

I said, "That's not true. The letter for his sister was in my letter; there was a piece of paper included there with clear instructions that went through the censor: 'Lubanya, please send this page on to my sister.' I sent it on to his sister. Then she wrote back to him, 'Petya, thank you very much for the letter.' So you all drew the conclusion that he must have gotten a letter out to his sister illegally. You don't have the right to punish him for having sent such a letter, all the more so because you don't have that letter in hand. So you think it over: you know that you don't have the right to do this." To which I added, "I'm filing a complaint against you."

Once I had left, I went to the commandant overseeing Chita Oblast. He received me very well. He was about 45 years old, a non-Russian. I told him everything—the whole story: that we are Christians, that we love the Lord and that there is now a war against our convictions, against our faith…. "…And now because of this they are eliminating people. By using these methods, though, you cannot kill off faith in God, you won't do away with it: this will only make it stronger as it grows up in our hearts."

He listened to me for a long time. I told him how they had treated my husband in the transfer prison: how they had grabbed him by the shoulders and slammed him into a radiator, after which he was in a very bad way.

He listened for a long time to all of this, then said, "That just cannot be. I cannot believe this. And I can't believe that you've come several thousand kilometers to tell this story."

I told him, "My husband is dying. He's not taking any food."

"How do you know?" he asked.

I explained to him, "In our last meeting, my husband told me that they intended to eliminate him. 'So,' he said, 'if they put me in segregation,[108] I'm not going to take any food.' I am sure that some people have thought up this punishment to eliminate him. Therefore, I implore you, please take the right course of action—the righteous course of action—concerning my husband."

He called the prison and asked where [prisoner] Rumachik was located. They answered, "In punishment segregation."

"What for?"

"Because he sent a letter illegally."

He answered, "Do you have this letter in your possession?"

"No."

"Then how do you know that he did this?"

"His sister wrote it."

"The fact that his sister wrote this is one thing," the commandant replied, "but you must have this illegal letter in hand. Then you can punish him. Release Rumachik *right now,* and punish whoever put him in there."

This was the fifteenth day of his confinement. On the fifteenth day he was set free. He didn't take any food for all 15 days. Moreover, he was also in frightening conditions: the cell was cold, and he couldn't sleep since the bunk was made of solid iron with bands at the head, feet and midsection. This sleep deprivation and lack of food had a profound effect on him. In this way they tried to eliminate him; they gave him a 15-day sentence four times: 60 days they gave him! It is clear that they were trying to kill him.

---

[108] Solitary confinement

But as Peter Vasilyevich told me during one of our visits: "Lubanya, our God is never late. He does everything on time." If I had come any later, it is clear that he would have died. But when I came, he was at least still able to move around, even though he had to hold himself up against the wall to do so. After that, he was laid up in the hospital for a very long time with a fever.

At that time, we were permitted "common visitation": that means that he sits in one booth while I sit in an opposing booth separated by a pane of glass. We have to talk through telephones so as to improve the quality of the tape recording of our conversation and so that it would be listened in on very well.

They didn't want to give me these visitation rights because he was in such a terrible condition and they didn't want him to tell me anything. Nonetheless, I replied, "It is the appointed time that we are permitted to have visitation. Please give me visitation rights." They refused. I went to the prosecutor, and the prosecutor said, "Have them give you a written refusal. We need something more than their spoken word to go on." I went to them and said, "Please give me the refusal in writing: the prosecutor demands it."

They replied, "We will give you visitation rights for two hours."

"Why two?" I asked. "Why not four?"

"We won't give you four."

"You will give me four," I replied.

They changed the "2" written on the sheet to "4," and gave me visitation for four hours.

You can't imagine what it was like. When I went into the booth, my husband was already waiting there. He was in an awful state and terribly thin. The telephone receiver was bound against his cheek with bandages.[109] I prayed, "Oh, Lord, just give the strength not to break down and cry." I didn't want him to see me dejected and crying. My heart was heavy. I said

---

[109] That is, he was too weak to hold the telephone receiver on his own.

to him, "Hello, Petyenko! Hello!"[110] His eyes were filled with tears. I said, "Praise the Lord that we can see each other again!" We stood, prayed out loud, sat back down, and began talking to each other by phone. Of course, there were people sitting all around us listening in, writing everything down, watching us closely to see what hand motions we used to describe ourselves. My husband was able to tell me everything, though, and we were able to communicate all we needed.

The work on the women's committee—or what we called the "Council of Prisoners' Relatives"—was very intense, very difficult and very dangerous. At any moment we could be arrested, but we decided to work anyway as a shield to our brethren and sisters. Our work became ever the more difficult, and once at one of our meetings the question was raised as to whether I would consent to be a "mail box"; that is, to have all the government's responses to our many petitions come to me on behalf of the persecuted brethren and sisters in our land. This was a frightening proposition, since I could be put in a psychiatric hospital for this activity, and they could take away my children and put them in an orphanage. Laying my hope on the Lord, however, I answered, "Yes, I am prepared to do this. We are already lying on the altar, there is nothing left for us but to be burned."[111] After I became the "mail box," the operatives of the KGB began to pressure and attack us even more strongly. They began to call me in to various places, but I didn't go to any of them. Once, three large men came to my apartment and asked, "Why is it that you're writing all these lies in your telegrams? That it's bad in such-and-such city, hither and yon, and so on…."

I said, "I write only the truth. I am a member of the Council of Prisoners' Relatives, and I have submitted my address so that all the answers from the

---

[110] Petyenko is a diminutive of Peter. Compare English, "Petie." The greeting style here sounds exceptionally warm and cheery in the original. The greeting used is the common Christian greeting, which is distinct from the usual Russian greeting we would find here among unbelievers.

[111] It is somewhat unclear as to whether the author intends to make reference to this passage, but it is worth noting Philippians 2:15–18 "That ye may be blameless and harmless, the sons of God, without rebuke, in the midst of a crooked and perverse nation, among whom ye shine as lights in the world; Holding forth the word of life; that I may rejoice in the day of Christ, that I have not run in vain, neither laboured in vain. Yea, and if I be offered upon the sacrifice and service of your faith, I joy, and rejoice with you all. For the same cause also do ye joy, and rejoice with me.

government come to me. I lay my life on the line for my brothers and sisters, because I know that all those who write write only the truth. Let me tell you the case with my husband…." I told them about all these instances of lawlessness and then added, "…And this is exactly the way it is, both for him and for other Christians. That's why we have directed ourselves to the government, that they would stop all this lawlessness."

They began to threaten me, saying, "We'll throw you in jail."

I replied, "Don't threaten me, please. I'm already ready. I've got a bag sown up with all my necessities packed. I'm ready to go."

They were obviously not expecting such a response, and they just stared at me, wide-eyed.

I had given myself into the Lord's hands, and you know, the Lord gave me such tranquility that they could not frighten me, and they were ashamed. I added, "Don't ever call me in again, because I won't come. I am blameless before you."

They answered, "Fine, Lubov Vasilyevna, we'll leave our phone number so that you can call in to tell us that you won't come in."

"No," I said, "I don't need your phone number, because I'm not coming in." So they left ashamed.

Of course, after this I felt so much pressure that I could not even go freely to the store. They followed me in packs. Once I decided to go to Moscow: I sat down on city transportation and could immediately feel that there were people—KGB operatives—going with me. I could already tell who they were by their clothing and all their mannerisms. I got on the *elektrichka*. How good that I was able to get in the first car; and one of them got on behind me. I decided suddenly to jump back out, and he jumped out behind me. I got back on, then he got back on. I jumped out again, and he jumped back out—except this time the door closed on his foot. It was good that we were in the first car, because the driver saw this and opened the door for him. I said to him, "Why are you running after me as if I'm some kind of criminal? What do you people want from me?" But he remained silent.

I got back on the *elektrichka* and went to the store; and he got on behind me and went to the store. I got on the bus, and he got on the bus. I got off the bus, and he got off the bus. Wherever I went, there he went, too. In this fashion he took me all the way home. It was so hard to bear all this that even now it's hard to talk about. It was hard even just to move.

Once when I was coming home [from services] late at night, I felt that there was someone following me. I decided not to go home by way of the *elektrichka*, but instead to try to lose the people tailing me. So I went by *marshrutka*[112] the absolute opposite way heading away from home, and they followed me the whole time by car…[I wasn't able to shake them, however,]…and they were with me all the way home. The Lord protected me, though, from whatever evil they might have done to me.

■ ■ ■ ■ ■

DURING THESE MOST DIFFICULT YEARS, they began to add on years to the prison terms our Christian brothers were serving. Without even letting them return home, they were adding on up to three years: someone might have one year added; someone else, two; yet another, three years. At this time, my husband's term was coming to an end. I thought, "Since they're already adding on prison time to the terms of the others, they're probably going to extend my husband's term as well."

Notwithstanding, my son Pavel and I decided to go to our husband and father for his release. I bought a bouquet of flowers—as I remember, it was a white bouquet of gladiolas. Pavlik asked, "Mama, can I buy a bouquet of flowers for papa, too?"

I said, "Sure, son. Let's buy a bouquet for you, too."

We bought two bouquets and went to the prison, but when we arrived they told us, "He is not here. They've transferred him to another area."

"Why? What for?" we asked.

"They're going to extend his sentence."

And so this expected time of meeting became a time of separation.

When I later met with the lawyer, he said to me, "Do you know what he's being tried for?"

"No," I replied.

---

112 Marshrutka: A type of public transportation. A mini-bus that follows a set path but that does not make predetermined stops. Because this is generally more comfortable than riding a bus or tram, passengers pay a higher fee for use than they would on trams, trolleybuses and buses.

"Political crimes. Here, read what they're trying him for...." He gave me the document, and as I read it my heart sank. The tears began flowing: the proscribed term was horrible—five years of incarceration followed by 7 years of [internal] exile. That made for a term of 12 years. This meant that, since he would have 12 years added onto the term of five that he had just served, we would be separated for a total of 17 years this time.

I turned to the Lord in prayer—tears in my eyes—and said, "Lord, help my husband, my children and me: give us strength and patience. Thy will be done."

Once the trial began, it lasted over a month. The prosecutor asked that he be given five years in prison and three years' exile. That meant 8 years. In my heart I said, "Praise God! Not 12 years, but only 8." But the judge commuted the sentence to five years' imprisonment. I thanked God again: "Praise God!" I said. "Already, it's not 8 years, but now only 5." With that, I threw him the bouquet of flowers. Other women from the church were at the trial, and they threw their bouquets also, so that he was showered in flowers. He was even able to

Luba Rumachik surrounded by church youth with flowers upon her return from Peter Rumachik's trial in 1985. Instead of being released at the conclusion of his term, 5 more years were added, and Luba returned empty handed.

catch some of the flowers, and he took them with him all the way to the prison, where they were finally confiscated. I said, "Petya, this is for you, for your faithfulness to the Lord."

For the authorities, this was most disturbing: this was the first time in a trial that they had seen people throw flowers to the condemned. There was a lot of talk of this incident afterwards.

So my husband was going to be taken off to serve yet another his sixth term. During the recess, he said to me, "Luba, you know, they are using the evidence gathered in my case to prepare a criminal trial against you and condemn you as well." He was obviously very troubled by this, but I smiled as I answered him, "Petyenko, don't be troubled. Don't worry. We'll be suffering for the Lord together that way. And the Lord will give us strength, both to you and to me." I comforted him in that way.

Of course, [my cheeriness] did afford him some comfort, but he was clearly concerned: I had so many children, and if they put me in prison so that I was in prison and so was he, then what would become of our children? At this time, they were already taking children away and throwing their mothers in prison.

A little time passed, and I was summoned to appear at the prosecutor's office. I did not go. I had told them, "I am innocent before you, therefore, I will not appear before you." Then the investigator came to me at my apartment and said, "Lubov Vasilyevna, you must appear *immediately* before the prosecutor."

I said, "Please give me a some time to speak to my family. You know, I don't want to go with you. I'll speak with you for a few minutes and then allow you to leave."

He left, and the children and relatives and I spoke for a few minutes to figure out what to do. I had such tranquility in my heart; and I was not alarmed. They said, "Go ahead and go. Maybe it's true that nothing will happen; otherwise, the Lord would have revealed it to us through His Spirit."

I said, "Maybe they're preparing a criminal case against me, and they want to ask about how I carried myself in Chita and what I talked about there."

So I decided to go. I didn't sleep all night, but instead spent the entire time getting all my things together in the event that I would be put in prison. Finally, I had my bag of necessities packed. In the morning I prayed in tears. I bid farewell to all the children and went with my sister to the Office of the Prosecutor. I took with me the sewn bag that I had prepared especially for prison.

…When I arrived at the prosecutor's office, he said, "Please, come in." I had set my bag down and the floor, and I picked it up to carry it into his office as I entered. He said, "You won't need your bag. What do you need your bag for? Leave it here."

"Maybe I'll have need of it."

"No, Lubov Vasilyevna. You won't need it."

I decided to take his word for it and left the bag there. As we entered the office, I said, "Please make this quick, since I have to catch the *elektrichka* back home."

He answered, "Lubov Vasilyevna, whoever comes to this office always leaves after a short while."

As I had expected, he really did begin asking me questions about the Chita case that, as my husband had already told me, had served as the basis for opening a criminal case against me. I answered him that this was all a lie, that this was all libel, and that I would not respond to anything written there. I said, "I am a Christian, and I cannot say those sorts of things: that I want to overthrow the government or that I am trying to do something else [subversive]."

He answered, "Very well. I will write [my superiors] back and inform them that we will not be taking this case, and that they should conduct any further inquiries themselves, as we are already inundated with cases." Then he added, "Lubov Vasilyevna, they really seem to be after you."

I said, "I know. The operatives of the KGB are trying to do only bad. They want to eliminate my husband, so here he is serving his sixth term. They gave him five years, and here now they want to put me in prison and take my children away. But you know, my life is in the Lord's hands. If He allows it, then they will imprison me. If not, then no one will arrest me." With that, we parted company.

■ ■ ■ ■ ■

OUR CHILDREN GREW UP WITHOUT their father. Whenever he was released from prison, he was only around for a short time before they would begin investigating his affairs again and he would have to go underground to labor for the Lord's glory.

Once when our daughter Valya was two years old she looked at me with her two inquisitive eyes and asked as we were sitting around the table with the other children, "Mama, what is a 'papa'? Is it a 'sapop'?" (A 'Sapop' is a kind of shoe.) The other children around the table laughed, and I was saddened by this, that my little girl didn't even know what a "papa" was.

Peter Rumachik and Luba in 1977 with their son Vova who did not recognize his father and is balking at greeting him.

She had grown up without a papa, and had just heard all the other children saying this word: "Papa," "papa." That's how all the children grew up. But praise God! He helped us in all difficulties.

Once when Petya came back from serving one of his prison terms, we were going to the worship service when he asked me a question: "Lubanya, tell me: Did you ever think to yourself: 'Now why did I ever marry Petya? I'm always living alone. He gets out of prison, leaves me with another child, and then goes back to prison. He gets out of prison, leaves me with yet another child, then goes back to prison…'." Truly, that [is the way it was,] and our children grew up without a husband and father. I would have really wanted my husband to take me to the maternity ward, and that he would be there to meet me when I got out…that we would be able to be together. But this almost never happened. Only rarely did things work out that way.

But I answered my husband: "No, Petyenko. I never had any thoughts whatsoever of being unhappy for having married you. I'm very thankful to the Lord for you: that I can strengthen you in the faith as my own faith is strengthened, and that I can be proud of such a husband that bears all these sufferings for the Lord's name."

Of course, this was difficult. There were times when I would get out of the maternity ward only to have my husband go underground that very day to labor for the Lord, since he was already under investigation. When our last son Vova[113] was born, for example, a full week passed from the time I was released from the maternity ward to the time my husband was arrested again.

Our church endured very strong persecutions from the authorities. We were unable to meet freely. We met in apartments and individual homes, and the authorities sought us out and broke up our meetings. They threw us out of these meetings, grabbing us by the hands and feet to throw us into the backs of vans to take us off into the forests. This happened nearly every time. We would meet in the forests: in the snow, in the rain, during bitter cold—and the love of God was aflame in our hearts. Our old women—some on crutches and canes—went into the forest. They were not afraid of the cold. Our youth went on ahead of them to clear the way in the snow.

The Lord helped us. We had an elder then, Aleksei Fedorovich, who always said,

> *Always count and remember the mercies of God*
> *Repeat them in your heart, one by one.*

This man, our pastor, died in prison for the name of the Lord.

Truly, as I look back on the path we've traversed with all its tribulations and sufferings, I am thankful to God—along with my children and my husband—that He never forsook us. He always helped us. This was in no small way through your prayers and material support. We thank you for your participation in our suffering.

Our life has still not yet ended on this earth. The Lord said, "[B]e thou faithful unto death, and I will give thee a crown of life."[114] We do not know what awaits us ahead, what trials and tribulations may be, but of this one thing we pray, that the Lord would help us to keep our faithfulness to Him to the end.

---

[113] A diminuitive of Vladimir.

[114] Revelation 2:10

We now have 6 children and 16 grandchildren. We would very much like to ask that you remember us in your prayers so that we—along with all our children and grandchildren—would all be in one ark of salvation together and that none of us would perish.

I have told the story of our life so that you might be strengthened in the faith yourselves as you see how the Lord allowed all these difficulties in our lives, but that we were able to bear all things. All of you: trust in the Lord. We do not know what tribulations may await you, but be faithful to God to the end. Do not fear. Do not doubt, for the Lord is always with us. He is faithful in His promise when He said, "I will never leave thee, nor forsake thee."[115] May the Lord help you to be strengthened in your faith and trust. Amen.

---

[115] Hebrews 13:5

If, after reading this account, you would be interested in finding out how you can have a part in helping meet the needs for building churches and spreading the Gospel in the former Soviet Union, please write or call BIEM at the address listed below:

Baptist International Evangelistic Ministries
P.O. Box 707
Danville, IN 46122-0707

Phone: 317-718-1633
FAX: 317-718-1693
Email: Missions@BaptistInternational.org

You may also visit our site on the World Wide Web at:
www.BaptistInternational.org

THE RETURN

Peter Rumachik's 2003 trip back to visit Chita and Perm,
where he suffered for the name of the Lord
(end of March – beginning of April 2003)

During the Christmas holiday season of 2002, I (Peter Rumachik) shared with my children and grandchildren how I desired some time before spring to visit the prison in Chita and those camps where the repressive Soviet regime sought to put me to death from 1981 to 1986. Then, on the way back to Moscow, I wanted to stop at the final camp in the Chusovsky Region of Perm Oblast. My children and grandchildren showed a lot of interest in this desire of mine, and they reminded me fairly frequently of the upcoming trip. My son Pavel also expressed his desire to accompany me to these forlorn places where the Lord had led me.

So it was that, armed with a camera and video recorder, plus some provisions for four days, I set off for Yaroslav train station in Moscow.[116] My son Pavel was supposed to arrive in Chita by plane six days after my departure.

Having situated myself in a comfortable train car and after making the acquaintance of my cabin mates, I started reading my Bible. Later, a conversation got going with my neighbors about God and eternal life. Among my traveling companions were people of various professions. One woman on her way to Vladivostok was a State Security agent.[117] I was with her all the way to my final destination in Chita. She listened more than any of the others about God, the Savior Jesus Christ, and eternal life.

Whenever you talk to people and tell them about the Gospel, you experience a pleasant sensation from being the sower of the good seed

---

[116] Since Tsarist times, the Yaroslav station has been the departure point of the Trans-Siberian railway, which connects Moscow with the Pacific port city of Vladivostok.

[117] That is, an agent of what was formerly known as the KGB: the acronym "K.G.B" stands for *Komitet Gosudarstvennoi Besopasnosti* (the Committee for State Security).

of love, peace, and happiness. Perhaps some day the seeds will grow up to produce good fruit. When I travel, I always take Christian literature with me and give it out to all who desire it. Even though our people were brought up in atheism for a long time, there remains in people an attraction toward the holy and the ethereal, and my cabin mates gratefully accepted New Testaments, tracts, and Christian booklets, promising to read them as they did so.

Snow-covered fields, forests, and villages flashed past the window of the train car, but in my heart memories welled up of past voyages in prison cars that were, as a rule, always filled to the brim. I studied the compartment I was in and thought of those days when soldiers would shove up to twenty-two men into a compartment normally designed for four to six. When it wasn't possible to push any more prisoners in, the soldiers would seize men by their hands and feet and throw them over the heads of the prisoners already in the compartment.

The soldiers gave us sardines or herring,[118] bread, and a little sugar. The lack of water was a huge problem. After we had eaten salted fish, our thirst was torturous, and the prisoners quickly gulped down their water ration. Whether this situation was premeditated or from a deficit of water, I don't know, but the soldiers did not provide any additional water.

Images welled up from those days of prison transfers, and it was painful to recall the uncensored language, where there were more curse words than clean ones. And so much smoke from the cigarettes of prisoners filled the compartment that it was unbearable. It was so hard in those conditions to begin to testify about God, a normal life, and eternal life. Nonetheless, one could find individual inmates who listened with great hunger to the Word of God and asked various questions that troubled their sinful souls.

The first stop that lay ahead on my 2003 journey was Perm intensive prison, where I had been held two times. There had been extremely strict rules there. From wake-up to lights-out, we were not allowed to lie down on our bunks. We couldn't even *sit* on them. And if we asked, "Why not?" then the answer we got from the guards was, "What? Are you asking to be

---

[118] Literally, the fish referred to here is *sprat (Clupea sprattus)*, which is a small species of European herring found in northeast Atlantic waters and is often canned as a sardine. ("Sardine" merely refers to any small fish canned in oil. There is no species of fish properly known as a sardine.)

put in isolation?" As a result, inmates lost the desire to question any more rules like that one.

The second intensive prison I visited was the one in Sverdlovsk, where I was detained four times. This was the most terrible of all the prisons where I had to be. They didn't give us mattresses there. The cells were so packed that it wasn't possible to step into them. So the soldiers just shoved the convicts in with their feet. If an inmate didn't manage to get his feet over the threshold, he risked having them crushed by the heavy metal door that the soldiers would slam shut with malicious contempt. This prison was the filthiest, the most infested with bed bugs. But even in these conditions the testimony of God had to go out. Further on were intensive prisons in Novosibirsk, Krasnoyarsk, Irkutsk and, finally, Chita. Each of these prisons has its own characteristic trademarks, and each of them had its own difficulties. But they also had their own joys connected with testifying divine truths—not only to inmates, but also to the guards and administrators.

When the train I was riding arrived in Chita, young Christian men and women were already waiting to meet me at the station. Then, as we were riding in their car through the city, one of the young people asked, "Have you ever been to Chita?"

"Yes," I said. "In the four years that I was in Chita, I was driven through the city many times, but I have never actually seen the city itself."

"How is that possible?" they asked me.

I explained that I had been driven around in a "Black Maria"[119] (a locked-down vehicle especially for prisoner transport). My youthful friends did not know that I had been in prison for four years there for the name of the Lord.

As I was speaking with the youth, we arrived at Antioch Baptist Church in Chita. Here I was met by a group of Christian youth. This was a joyous meeting, and I thanked God for those years I spent in the prisons and camps of Chita Oblast sowing the seeds of Truth and the love of Christ. At the time that I had been a prisoner in Chita, there was a small group of elderly Christians there, but there was not so much as a trace of Christian

---

[119] Literally, "Black Crow," in Russian. The term "Black Maria" has been used here as the closest slang equivalent in English to a prison transport vehicle of this type.

youth. Having met the youth that was here now, I told them my purpose for coming to Chita, and I told them that my son Pavel—who was supposed to be flying into Chita—and I did not have a place to stay. The youth quickly resolved the matter of our living arrangements, and about forty-five minutes later I found myself with the very hospitable family of Brother Vladimir and his wife Tatiana. This is a remarkable family that loves the Lord and His people. After I had a pleasant time of getting acquainted with the family and a good supper, God also gave a pleasant night's rest.

In the morning we went to worship services at the church. It was a delight for me to see that there were children of God in this city and to share with them my joy in fellowship together and ministry for the Lord. Afterwards, we had a pleasant discussion with the youth of the church.

As I was remembering the past, I rejoiced that God has established His church in this city and that it is growing and spreading the sweet fragrance of Christianity around itself. But some twenty years ago the KGB, along with the prison officials, tried to put me to death, and it was only through the mercy of God that I was able to endure and remain alive. I spent this entire Sunday in the company of children of God, surrounded by their attention and care. The next day I met my son Pavel, who arrived by airplane. We needed to receive permission to visit Chita Prison and two camps where I was detained from 1981 to 1986. We also wanted to visit the Oblast Court[120] and the Prosecutor's Office.

During the second half of the day we went to the office of the Directorate of Punishment and Corrections (UIN).[121] A captain[122] received us and asked us to write a declaration in which we expressed our purpose and reason for visiting the prison and two camps. We wrote the declaration and handed it to the captain, who explained that permission is given only

---

[120] In the American legal system, this would be roughly equivalent to the "district court," in this case presiding over an area slightly less than the state of California in size, with a population of about 1,295,000 (about 2,000 more than Idaho, according to US census, 2000.)

[121] Notice that, while this is essentially the same "department of corrections" that administrated the GULAG system, the GULAG is not mentioned here.

[122] Despite recent changes in many of Russia's institutions in the public sector, the penal system in Russia is still administered under military regulations and staffed by military personnel. For this reason, personnel who would be called "correctional *officers*" in the US are commonly referred to as "soldiers" in literature detailing Russian prison life.

by General Philippov.[123] When the captain led us in and introduced us to the general, telling him who I was and why we had come, the general perked up at the sound of my name. He began to ask clarifying questions.

"Isn't that the same legendary name I've heard so much about?" he said.

"What exactly have you heard?" I replied.

He explained that he had heard of a certain man by this name who had been held in isolation[124] for a very long time in the Chita camps, but when the time came for his release, this man had five more years of incarceration added to his sentence.

"That man you have been told so much about is the man standing before you."

Then the general invited us to sit. He said that he had many questions for us and that he was very happy to meet someone who had endured so much for his faith in God. After a pleasant conversation, the general wrote a single word on our declaration: "PERMITTED,"[125] and then added his signature.

He added verbally, "You may photograph and videotape everything you need, except for the forbidden zone and the guard towers around the prison perimeter. If the local administrators give you any grief, tell them they can call General Philippov."

We said a friendly goodbye to the general and left for our temporary quarters.

The next day I set off with Pavel to zone YAG-14/5, where I was interned from 1982 to 1985. In this zone they tried to kill me in a cold cell that was kept at three to four degrees above 0° Celsius—and they sentenced

---

[123] Based on the fact that Phillipov holds the rank of general, it is to be assumed that he administrates the correctional facilities for the entire oblast. Individual prisons are administered by colonels. Often, the individual concentration camp facilities would be grouped together, so that several camps might be under the command of a single colonel, with the appropriate ranks of officers administering the rest of the facility.

[124] Special punishment, usually in isolation

[125] Literally, "I permit [it]." This is expressed by one word in Russian.

me to 60 days. This was an isolation cell: very cold, and full of wood lice[126]. The window in this cell had no glass in it. At that time, there was frost on the ground outside. I fervently prayed to God with fasting that He would send His protection and aid. My body shook continually from the cold. It was simply impossible to fall asleep in those kinds of temperatures. I had to massage my arms and used physical exercise, but none of that helped to keep me warm. Bed linens were not issued to prisoners in isolation, and you were put in wearing nothing but light worker's dungarees (without

any head covering or boots), so it was impossible to get warm. But my God heard me and delivered me from that terrible dungeon on the fifteenth day.

Now I learned that that cell has been changed into a storeroom, so we were not able to see that terrible cell, that chamber of death. After

Prison block № 4, zone № 5, in Chita. I preached to these prisoners and prayed for them.

being held in that cell, I was laid up in the prison hospital for three and a half months, and God reinstated my health.

When Pavel and I entered the camp, we headed for the camp church that had been opened after *perestroika*. We had a pleasant meeting with brothers in Christ from among the prisoners who put their faith in Christ in camp. I got to know them and rejoiced that the Lord had regenerated them to salvation and had brought them into a new life in this very place where I had sown the seeds of God's Word, seeds of God's love.

In that fellowship I encouraged these believers with my son Pavel, here in this very place behind the barbed wire, giving them instruction.

---

[126] In prior translations, the very obscure term for "wood lice" was confused for "centipedes." The wood louse (properly a crustacean, not an insect) is commonly known as a *pill bug,* from its ability to roll its oblong, elliptical body into a ball.

They asked many questions, and I tried to answer them. I gave out a lot of Christian literature. Pavel was videotaping everything at this time with the video camera.

One inmate, a gypsy named Alek, sincerely prayed to ask forgiveness of his sins. Then a singing group praised the Lord on musical instruments and in song. At the conclusion of our fellowship I said a prayer of blessing for these people who had come to the Lord through suffering, and we bade a warm, heartfelt farewell to this prison church.

New souls came to Christ! The Gypsy Alek received Christ after having a conversation with me.

After that meeting, the officer accompanying us asked what else we would like to see. I answered that I wanted to see the fourth block, where I had been detained from 1982 to 1985. He said that this block consisted solely of young people and that "they probably won't want to listen to you." But once I heard that there were nearly 200 young people in that block, my desire to visit them was all the stronger.

When we stepped inside the block and greeted the men, we saw that all of these young detainees obviously mistook Pavel and myself for prison administrators, which only made sense because we looked like we were in charge. After all, it's not every day that a ranking officer accompanies visitors off the street through the prison.

But then I began to tell about how, some twenty years earlier, I was detained in this same facility, in this very block, and that I had served my term for my faith in God. That statement sparked a lot of interest, and soon we were surrounded by people on all sides who wanted to listen to us and ask questions. I took out my Bible and began talking about how, even though they were violators of man's laws, God loves them and wants to mend their lives and return them to a normal life with their families. I testified about how Christ the Savior loves them, their families, and all humanity. I spoke to them about how our life will continue after death, because man was created by God for eternity. I spoke about how there are two places in eternity: heaven and hell. But God loves sinners and saves them from eternal punishment and perdition. God wants every person to recognize himself as a sinner and, through repentance, to enter the Kingdom of God, eternal blessedness in Christ Jesus. This is the beautiful eternity God has prepared for people, but the Devil deceives people because he has worked them over, taken them captive in sins and torments them to this day.

"And your relatives and loved ones suffer as a result of your sinful life," I continued. I spoke to them about how, if they would believe and repent, then their lives would already change here on earth, so that they might be able to get parole and go home to a normal life with their families.

These young men were listening to me when suddenly one inmate obviously wanted to point out how he was special and announced, "I'm Muslim, so there are other ways for me to get to heaven."

I asked him his name, and whether he had committed sins like drinking vodka, cursing, smoking, and so on.

"Yes," he said openly.

"Then you are sinful as a Muslim, just like everyone else, and the label of 'Muslim' will not help you as far as salvation is concerned. You need to repent, just like the gypsy named Alek repented in the prison church."

I asked all the listeners to start reading the New Testaments that they could get from their friends—my brothers—at the prison church, and I encouraged them to that end. By reading the Word of God, they would come to faith, obtain real life, and find true happiness. During my discussion, Pavel took many photographs and taped with the video camera, and nobody interfered. When I suggested that we all have our picture taken together for a memento, many people tried to squeeze into the shot, and the man I had been talking to—the Muslim—squeezed in close beside me and stood right next to me. It was nice for me to stand next to him and to trust in the mercy of the Lord: that the seed sown would bring forth its fruit in due time, even in this person, too.

At the conclusion I asked the listeners if they wanted me to say a prayer of blessing for them, and they all answered in unison: "Yes!" So I said a prayer of blessing for them with outstretched hands, asking the Lord's mercy upon these young men who had fallen under the influence of the Devil.

When we finished the prayer, one of the convicts approached me and said that he knew me, that about twenty years ago he had been locked up here together with me. He also wanted to have his picture taken with me, and we bade a friendly farewell to these young, unhappy men. As we were leaving, they accompanied us along the street inside the prison yard and continued asking their questions, and we answered as best we could.[127] Later, I could still see the images flashing before me of their sad eyes, eyes that had for the first time received hope that not everything for them was lost. They had, perhaps, learned for the first time that God loves them. I was firmly convinced that the officer who had accompanied us there had been wrong when he said that there wasn't much chance that these young violators of man's laws would want to listen. How truly had the living words of John 1 spoken: "And the light shineth in darkness; and the darkness comprehended it not."[128]

As we were walking toward the prison mess hall, we suddenly heard someone shout, "Peter Vasilyevich, come over here."

We turned and saw a man standing by the gate to the general population area for the cell block. (All blocks are divided into local populations; this is the same way it was when I was incarcerated there.) When I walked up and greeted the man standing on the other side of the gate, he said that he recognized me. Truth be told, it was hard for me to recognize him, but it was a fact: I had seen him some twenty years earlier in this prison, and to my great sorrow, he still was here behind bars.

We exchanged opinions about life, and I urged him to accept Christ so that his life would acquire meaning and change for the better. When we parted, sad thoughts troubled me: that this man had spent all of his life in prison. And for what? For the fact that he had not wanted to receive

---

[127] This is an especially touching picture, given the Russian cultural context: In a formal setting like this, it would be expected for the prisoners to let their guests leave without further ado, once they had said their goodbyes. Yet here we see that the prisoners are truly hungry for answers, truly thirsting for the truth, because they break the cultural norms to continue asking questions.

[128] John 1:5. Here the KJV contains a word usage that has changed over time: "Comprehended" here corresponds closely to the modern word, "*apprehended.*" This usage is retained in the Russian translation. The idea is, "And the light shineth in darkness; and the darkness *did not overpower it.*"

God's Truth. God says in His Word, "And you will know the truth, and the Truth shall set you free" (John 8:32).

Next we visited the food service area, the kitchen, and the bakery. We spoke with the cooks and bakers, declaring the mercy of God that had been revealed in Jesus Christ to perishing sinners. I have to give credit where it is due, that the food for the inmates, especially the bread that they cook at the prison, is much better than when I was incarcerated. The cooks told us that people on the outside say that prison fare is about like the food in a third-class restaurant; and that is true. Of course, we wanted to sample the skill of the prison chefs for ourselves, so we headed off to the cafeteria. Here for three years I had daily received food so poor in quality that the very smell of it drove all appetite away. Truly, much has changed in our prisons in the last decades, including the food.

Then we headed toward where the isolation cell had been, where I was thinking I would find that terrible cell in the holding block where

In Perm prison camp 36, I spent 11 days in solitary punishment. Inside the cell it was damp. The temperature was no higher than +3° or +4° Celsius.

the KGB had tried to kill me through the camp administration. This cell had been bitterly cold: roughly +3 to +4 degrees Celsius, and I was given sixty days of incarceration in that isolation cell. I was put in isolation so that no witness would see when I died from the cold.

As we walked down the corridor that the cell was on, my heart involuntarily tensed up from the memory of what I had lived through, and shivers ran through my body from those horrors that I had to survive enclosed within the walls of this chamber. I do not know if it is fortunate that we could not see that cell, since it had been refurbished into a storage unit for the personal effects of the condemned. But as the guard opened the door to that room, my heart involuntarily skipped a beat from the memory of those experiences. I told the officer and the quartermaster that were with us of how people had tried to kill me in this cell, but the Lord came to my aid, and I was released from that cell on the fifteenth day.

As we were walking past the camp cultural center, I recalled how I had been tried there in 1986 after I had already served my five-year sentence and yet was not released. The Devil through his servants decided to continue his plan for putting me to death. The camp administration had told me openly, "Either you will deny your God and your religious propaganda, or we will kill you with punitive isolation."

Especially zealous in this endeavor were three individuals: the assistant director of Regimental Operational Work, Captain Nedorezov; and the Director of Operations ("Senior Godfather" in Russian prison slang) Major Lisitsky; and "Junior Godfather" Lieutenant Palkin. But my God did not allow that foul plan to happen, but instead stopped the jaws of these predators. Even though they added on five years, I served only a year and a half— so that on February 5, 1987, by decree of the Presidium of the Supreme Soviet I was amnestied even though I did not request it.

I was kept in this cell for three days during the trial in 1986. The floor was cement, and the window was blocked with metal shutters, so light did not penetrate that gloomy cell. I was not given any bedding. They kept me there in order to break my will, to keep me from testifying about God during the trial, but the Lord strengthened me.

Now, twenty years later, I was standing at this very cultural center and remembering that crooked court and Judge Simonov, who fabricated my case with the participation of the senior investigator for especially sensitive affairs under the Chita municipal prosecutor's office (in actuality KGB Investigator Natalia Titova). This was where they held a trial, which was nothing but a mockery of law; because even if the law was bad, laws still existed in the USSR. For two weeks the mockery of my person and conscience continued, and then they transferred the proceedings to the largest auditorium in the Chita Oblast Court. Three weeks later, an atrocious verdict was passed against me: five years of hard labor in prison camps. But my God, by whom I live, did not allow the servants of the Devil to put me to death. So, as I look back on everything, I want to say again, "Our God is great, and under His shelter a man is secure and happy!"

Two officers who had been block commanders in this prison zone recognized me.

Once we had bidden farewell to this gloomy prison, Pavel and I returned to Chita. Our next stop was another camp: YAG 14-1. This prison camp is located in the city of Nerchinsk in Chita Oblast. We arrived in Nerchinsk early the next morning and immediately headed to the prison. Since the warden had not arrived yet, the staff did not let us enter the general population area. When the warden arrived, we received permission to enter, but were not allowed to take the video camera with us.

One of the warden's lieutenants accompanied us. He was a young, educated man, who was pleasant to talk to. We asked him questions concerning his belief in God. (Incidentally, he didn't deny the reality of God.)

When we walked into the prison area, we saw three convicts, who greeted us. We were continuing down the road, when suddenly one of the convicts started timidly hurrying toward us, all the while studying me intently.

"Peter Rumachik," he blurted, "is that really you?"

"Yes, it's me." Of course, I didn't recognize the man, so I asked, "And who are you?"

Pointing to the name tag on his chest, he said, "I'm Sergei Zhilin."

This clarification didn't bring anything about him to memory. Then he asked me if I remembered when he was held in punitive segregation in Chita with me some twenty years earlier. Then I truly recalled when we pulled into Nerchinsk station... I remembered a certain cell where they put me, and that there was a man there who sat up all night trying to prove to me that there is no God, and that He will not help me in anything. I had even told my son Pavel about this episode on the way here. Now here was this same man, standing before us.

I reminded Sergei again of our talk in the cell: that there *is* a God, who not only protected me, but also took me out unharmed on the second day from between the walls of that terrible place. My God protected me (in spite of the dishonest people who had thought to put me to death). He not only protected me, but He set me free before my prison term was up.

"And here I am before you, healthy and unharmed." Then I asked him if he had accepted Jesus as his Savior.

He somewhat apprehensively stepped closer to me and said quietly, "I have a pocket full of diplomas from theological seminaries, but I will tell you in spite of that: there is no God."

His convict friends and the officer accompanying us heard this discussion. Of course, what I heard took my breath away, and I expressed nothing but sorrow for his statement. Nonetheless, I expressed interest in how much time he had left until the end of his term. He replied that his release was still thirteen years away. I pitied this man, and I told him how my heart was pained. I don't know whether it was my sympathy or a direct act of God's power that worked on this man, but he continued walking around the rest of the prison zone with us. He saw and heard a lot from how we talked to the other inmates and probably drew his own conclusions.

As we were walking further through the camp, a corporal approached us and asked us to go to the administration and pick up the video camera that we had not been allowed to bring into the facility. It was obvious that the warden had telephoned General Phillipov, who was not happy with the warden's restriction. Pavel returned to the main administration of the camp and picked up our video camera; then we continued our journey through the prison camp. We visited the mess hall, the library, and the prayer room. I was pleasantly surprised that the library had a shelf of Christian literature, with Bibles, New Testaments, and Christian journals. Any one of the inmates could freely take and use all of these.

Twenty years ago I couldn't have imagined that someday there would be Bibles in this prison just lying about, free for the taking. At that time, my Bible had been confiscated and placed in storage, and it was in this particular camp where Captain Nedorezov and Major Lisitsky had offered me a quick and easy path to my release: only if I would deny God and stop preaching the Gospel. *These* were the people who had constantly confined me in frigid punitive segregation cells because I ignored their suggestions and testified everywhere about Christ Jesus.

But now, twenty years later, the seeds sown for God's Kingdom had yielded their fruit. God gave the opportunity in these places of detention for people to access the saving Gospel, while my persecutors are in their "earned respite"—their pensions. One of those persecutors, Major Lisitsky, lives in a village not far from the camp. Of course, I have forgiven these people, because I cannot—and I have no right—to take revenge against them. God is their judge, and He tells me along with all Christians to forgive our enemies and to pray for them, to love them and do them well. If, after that, they do not repent of all the wicked deeds and do not understand all the evil for which they are accountable before God and men... then they will not escape the just judgment of God, which will be as coals of fire heaped upon their heads.[129]

In the library of the Chita prison there are now Bibles, New Testaments, and other Christian literature. Sergei Zhilin followed our group through the prison.

I was allowed to give Christian literature to the prisoners.

The camp "prayer room" was outfitted in Russian Orthodox style. The walls were adorned with images, and the man in charge of the room explained to us that all of the icons had been painted by inmates. Three Orthodox priests had come and blessed everything according to Orthodox custom.

Looking around at the images, I asked, "What is this icon here, the one with a picture of a baptism being performed through pouring?"

The man in charge explained, "That's the baptism of Jesus Christ."

"Did the priests bless that one, too?" I inquired.

---

[129] Almost certainly a reference to Proverbs 25:22, though Psalm 140:10 seems to better capture the author's meaning here, where a similar expression is used.

"Yes."

Sergei Zhilin, who was following right on our heels, asked us to go into the PTU (Production-Engineering Directorate), where the inmates are taught a trade. Sergei is in charge of this school. We were pleasantly surprised when we saw tomato plants growing in the rooms of the PTU, with mature fruit on the vines. It was the beginning of March, which is a very early time of year to be doing this sort of thing. But Sergei explained that they have a greenhouse where he harvests tomatoes, and that the work brings him joy and satisfaction. This man has aspirations to a normal life, but the reality of such a thing behind barbed wire is a very complicated matter.

We looked over the PTU and saw that there was at least something to keep the inmates going, and for those who had no profession, they could acquire one here in prison camp. Sergei was touched by our attention to him, and as a token of gratitude handed us two souvenirs. In my time, it had been strictly forbidden to bring in or take out souvenirs or artifacts from prison facilities.

"Do you mean to tell me that nowadays you can actually give and receive souvenirs?" I asked.

The officer accompanying us replied, "Yes, you may."

Continuing on, we came to a building where I had been detained for a year and a half, from 1981 to 1982. This was cell block № 1, where there were mainly murderers and people working for Operations (snitches), or as the convicts called them, the "Godfather's" operatives.[130] That had been an altogether tough time for me, since I was constantly being held in punitive separation cells, and these operatives were watching my every step and reporting it to the administration. One time the director of Operations, Major Lisitsky, told me with poisonous irony, "I'm watching every step you take, and I know everything about you, down to how many times you go to the latrine."

---

[130] Note that the use of Russian prison slang is different from the English usage: In English, the term "Godfather" is often associated with the Italian Mafia. In the Russian sense, the "Godfather" refers to the prison administrator in the role of *spymaster*. In this sense, the Russian usage is not dissimilar to the English: The warden of the prison is seen in a role similar to a *don*.

Just to see if he was bluffing, I asked, "Tell me: How many times did I go to the latrine today?" He stated a number that was dead on. I was surprised at his zeal, and commended him for his investigative efforts.

Now, when we approached the cell block, I asked the officer accompanying us for permission to go inside. He didn't refuse, but he warned us

Chita Prison № 1. Now the prisoners can see the sky from inside their cells because the metal shutters were removed in 2002.

that at that time there were 200 men being held there who were sick with an open form of tuberculosis. Of course, in that case we decided not to enter the block and limited ourselves to a photograph by the fence around the local zone. While we were taking the photograph, a few dozen miserable convicts strolled over to the fence, and I explained to them why we were getting our picture taken here. I tried to share a few words from the Bible and personally from myself, so as to somehow comfort them by giving them hope in Jesus Christ.

We next walked to the alert unit (the duty unit), which was located on the second floor. From here, the entire zone was visible as if it were in the palm of your hand. Major Lisitsky had interrogated me in this room many times, and I always answered with silence. Here he would write the order to put me into the punitive separation cell. Once he tried to beat me here, but my God helped me: suddenly—and unexpectedly for both of us—the chief duty officer for that zone came in, leaving Major Lisitsky no option but to desist in his aggressive behavior toward me.

The door from that room opened onto the flat roof of the building, which was right up against the duty unit. We could see the entire prison zone from that spot, and as we stood there I recalled horrors from my past life, like the time soldiers quickly took up positions with mini-guns[131] and opened fire on the entire zone. (Fortunately, they were firing blank rounds.) Meanwhile, dozens of other soldiers stormed into the zone armed with metal-reinforced shields, police batons, and guard dogs. With screams in their throats, they pushed toward their artillery-guarded objectives. Meanwhile, the best thing for unfortunate convicts to do was to hide under their beds so as to not fall into the hands of a soldier. At times like these, under the guise of "training," soldiers would simply beat inmates, and this was considered a normal occurrence in Soviet prisons.

Back in the present, Sergei asked me to say a prayer for him, and I joyfully agreed. Later, I asked about his plans for his life. He answered that his thinking had changed for the better, and that these changes had taken place in his heart during our trip around the facility. He promised that he would try to live according to the will of God and normal human behavior.

After Pavel and our guide and I parted company with Sergei, we set off in the direction of the building where the punitive segregation (special punishment) cells were located. On the way, we met a prisoner who recognized me, and I remembered him as well. Just as before, he was working as a cobbler, repairing the shoes of inmates for free. Had this man been living in freedom, he could have been living well, making stylish modern footwear, but sin and crime had made him a slave, both physically and spiritually. In our discussion, we talked about that, and I reminded him of how his life would change and he would have happiness in his personal life if he would repent and receive Jesus Christ.

In punitive segregation we looked into a few cells, and my past days in these gloomy cells came back to me, the years when I was under the same weight as these misfortunates. That had been like a nightmarish dream. But I was happy that I had also sown the seeds of God's love and God's Word in Nerchinsk.

---

[131] Large machine guns, usually mounted, though technically a "mini-gun" may not necessarily be mounted. The term "mini-gun" has been chosen here in the translation as it conveys a sense of size. (I.e., the guns mounted on attack helicopters). A typical example of what the author probably has in mind would be the Degtyarev-Shpagin (DShK) 12.7 mm, weighing 148 kilograms (325 lbs) fully loaded, and dispersing 600 rounds per minute. The DShK could have been in service during 1981–2 in the Soviet Army.

Afterward, we went to see the administrator of the camp, Colonel Marchuk. He was about seventy years old and had been assigned to this position after I had already been released. During our discussion he said that not a single officer was left in the camp from the time that I was detained there. Some had retired. Others had been fired. I inquired about Major Lisitsky, and he responded that the major was retired and living in a village not far from the prison. He told us the address where we could find him.

I asked the colonel if he believed in God, and whether he was preparing to go into the next world. Obviously, he hadn't been expecting that sort of question, and after thinking for a long time and choosing his words carefully, he replied that he *did* believe. Of course, we delicately bade him not to abuse his power over these unfortunate men (the inmates), and reminded him that there is a greater power of God over us, and that the time will come for the colonel to give an account to God for his life and actions. He did not resist our reminders.

After we thanked the warden and his lieutenant who had accompanied us around the prison zone, Pavel and I walked out of the prison camp. We decided to take a picture of ourselves as a memento against the backdrop of the camp. Just at that moment, a lady officer strolled up to us (she was Buryat[132] by nationality). She asked us some personal questions. We amicably answered them, and then it was our turn to ask a few questions about her faith in God. She replied that she believed in God, but in her heart.

There was about an hour left before our bus was to leave, so we decided to pay a visit to retired Major Lisitsky. We found the apartment without any great effort and rang the doorbell. From behind the door a pleasant, aged woman's voiced called, "Who is it?"

"Friends," we replied.[133] She began to open the door to us with great caution, all the while asking who we were and why we had come.

---

132 The Buryats are an Asiatic nationality in southern Siberia. Traditionally, Buryats are Buddhist, having more historical and religious ties with China than Russia.

133 Literally, "Your own." This simple expression has no real equivalent in English, and so has been rendered as, "Friends." It is, in fact, considerably more intimate than the term "friends" conveys.

We asked permission to step into her home, so that we could explain who we were and what we were doing there. When we had entered, I asked, "Is Vladimir Mikhailovich at home?"[134]

She answered that he was not home, but had gone to Chita and would only be back tomorrow. Then, as she looked attentively at me, she said, "I recognize you."

This surprised me, since she and I had never met before. So I asked, "How is it that you could recognize me?"

"Not long ago we were looking at pictures and remembering about you."

So I asked again, "What kind of clothing was I wearing in the photograph, civilian or prison clothes? And what was the occasion that you were remembering me?"

She explained that the photograph in their possession showed me in civilian clothes and said, "Our recollection of you was positive."

I asked her, "Do you believe in God?"

"Yes. My husband and I read the Bible, but my husband is more diligent at it."

I was touched by this testimony and by the change in the retired major. God truly does His work in the life of

I met with lawyer Ludmila Aleksandrovna Belkina at her home. We recalled how I was tried in 1985–1986. She leafed through the file that she had created at the beginning of the trial, and then presented it to me. She believes in God; I urged her to receive Christ soon so that we would meet again, but next time in Heaven.

every man. We expressed our sorrow that we were not able to meet up with her husband. I then took out a copy of *Our Daily Bread* and wrote on the flyleaf: "To the former director of the Operations Unit, Major V. M. Lisitsky, a gift from ex-convict P. V. Rumachik. I have forgiven you for everything and very much desire to meet you again in Heaven. If you find time and wish to write me, I would be glad to receive your letter." After jotting my

---

[134] Asking for "Vladimir Mikhailovich" is, while formal, considerably more intimate than asking for him by last name.

home address and telephone number, I added, "Till we meet again!" After giving the book to Vladimir Mikhailovich's wife and saying goodbye, we left for the bus stop.

We attended worship services at the church in Nerchinsk. They received us there very hospitably and asked us to share a word. I spoke about how, some twenty years ago in a Nerchinsk prison camp I had sown the seeds of God's Word; about how they tried to put me to death there, but God—who had sent me there in the first place—was my Shield and my Aid.

"All the plans of the adversaries were thwarted, and as a result God founded your church. Now you can visit this prison camp and continue that work, which God began through me in the past."

I thanked God for His great and wonderful works. Later, a few people from the church accompanied us to the train, and we returned to Chita without incident. Ahead of us lay the daunting task of finding a certain prosecutor through whom God delivered my life from death. His name was Yuri Nizhniy. With great difficulty we learned at the prosecutor's office that in the summer of 1982 he had left his job there voluntarily, and that his present address was unknown. I was sorry that we could not see this kind and just man, but there was no way to change anything.

After this, we visited Chita Oblast Court. The workers there received us very well, and we were even allowed to take our pictures against the backdrop of the courthouse. The court clerk explained to us that this was a new courthouse, and that the old building in which I had been tried had been transferred to some communal venture; but she gave us the address of the old courthouse building. I then asked if I might be able to look through the files of the case under which a five-year term was added onto my sentence without release in 1986 after I had already served a five-year term. The clerk answered that I could see the file if it had not been destroyed.

She then started telephoning around and spent a long time compiling notes. Finally, she said that my file had been destroyed. Of course, this was a lie. We later found out from the prosecutor's office that my case file was in the offices of the FSB[135] for Chita Oblast, and on the last day of our stay

---

135 The FSB is the new name of the KGB.

in Chita we were granted permission to acquaint ourselves with this nightmarish case. (Before we could see the file, we had to give a written affidavit saying that we would not take revenge against those who had slandered me. Truth be told, we couldn't read through the whole case, which consisted of three volumes. All together they totaled about 500 pages. An FSB agent explained to us that we could return any time to continue getting familiar with the material, but that it might be forwarded to the FSB archives in the city of Omsk.

When we left there, we located the old building of the Chita Oblast Court. The chief administrator of the venture that is housed there now led us into an office that was once the largest auditorium in the court. It used to hold 300 people. That chamber has now been converted into three rooms.

I could visually pick out the places where the judges, the prosecutor, and the defense had sat, and where, behind a barrier and under heavy guard, I was kept. I was saying all this out loud as I worked it through in my mind, and the young women who worked for the venture stood up and listened. I explained to them that I had been tried for my faith in God, and that when I was sentenced to five years of hard labor in the concentration camps, my brothers and sisters in the faith threw me flowers, even though it was cold winter outside. In this way, our brothers and sisters expressed the strongest of protests against the Soviet court.[136]

I recalled how the judges snatched up their briefcases in panic and fled from their seats in great haste, while the soldiers guarding me crawled around on the floor trying to collect all the flowers. The soldiers had been given the command that I was not to take a single flower back with me to prison. But of course, I wanted very much to pick up and keep these flowers of brotherly love from God's people. That joy was taken from me, too. Yet, I managed to keep one flower and took it all the way back to the cell, where the inmates and I rejoiced as we examined the beauty of God's creation. We often don't notice the beauty of flowers; but there in the sullen, soiled prison, people go for years without seeing a flower. So for them this was

---

[136] That is, by throwing flowers, they were *congratulating* the condemned for his conviction: in effect saying that the Soviet court is so crooked that a conviction by such a court is really an *honor*.

a miracle to enjoy. And we rejoiced, even though they had given me five more years of hard labor in the camps.

The next day Pavel and I planned to visit Chita prison, the so-called facility IZ75-1, where I was kept for 14 months. At the outset, we were introduced to a journalist reporting on prison affairs. (The journalist was a young woman.) She interviewed me about all the events connected with my being in this prison and about how it was that I, at a young age in Soviet times, came to believe in God.

After that, they introduced us to the warden of the prison, a colonel whose name I don't remember. Once we had exchanged pleasantries, he asked me if I remembered him.

"No, I don't remember you."

He explained to me that some twenty years ago he had seen me at the prison in Nerchinsk, to which he had come on assignment from the Directorate.[137]

"Why didn't you ease my situation, if you had come from the Directorate?" I asked.

He explained that at that time, the people handling my case wore *big* stars on their epaulets, but he had only *little* stars at the time. After a few questions, he allowed us to visit the prison, but did not permit us to take our camera with us.

We walked through an entrance area into the general population zone. The first thing that caught our attention was that there were no iron slats on the windows. Now convicts could gaze out to the prison yard and see the sun and blue sky.

The assistant warden in charge of the educational unit accompanied us. I asked him to take us to the building where I had been detained when I was given five more years. But unfortunately—or fortunately, perhaps— that building turned out to be in hazardous condition: The outside wall was falling apart, and we could see inside the four-story building that there were metal beds with no mattresses. We stood at a distance from this building, and I told about how a certain man on death row who was being held in the basement corresponded with me by "string" mail. After four months, this

---

[137] That is *the* Directorate: on assignment from the governing body of the GULAG concentration camp system itself. This would have been quite an impressive credential at the time.

man sincerely repented of his sins, and when I received his letter drenched with the tears of repentance, I likewise wept for joy. How many unhappy people, deceived by Satan, perished and perish still in these prison houses! How they need the Gospel light, God's Word. And my God gave me the privilege of bringing the message of salvation to these unhappy souls.

We visited the basement, where the punitive segregation cells had been. Now this is where the people with life sentences are held. We could see through the window (where the food is given) one middle-aged man who had been sentenced to life imprisonment. He was pensive, with a downcast face, in a half-darkened cell. He ate his lunch without any hurry.

My heart was profoundly saddened by this sullen picture. Two or three cells down from that one was an empty cell, and I asked for it to be opened. This cell reminded me of when, after the trial in 1986, I was placed in punitive isolation just to sap my strength for answering questions in a way that they found unpleasant during the trial.[138] Pavel photographed me in this cell. Perhaps I had spent three sleepless nights there [in the similar cell where I had been previously detained].

I then asked them to open a cell that had men in it. That cell confined about forty men, all roughly middle-aged. I greeted the detainees, introduced ourselves, and explained why I had asked for this cell to be opened. I then expressed my sorrow that these people were in prison.

During the course of this dialogue, many questions were directed at me. A few detainees had quite aggressive attitudes and tried to convince me that rather than talking to them, I should be talking to the *administration* about God, sin, and living a just and holy life. I agreed with them, since according to God all had sinned before Him. I bade them look into their own hearts and to look into the Word of God (since the prison had a Bible,

---

138 Although the wording in Russian clearly states what has been translated here, the timing seems off. It would make more sense if the author had said either, "I was put in the cell *before* the trial, in order to sap my strength for answering questions the authorities might find unpleasant," or, "I was put in the cell *after* the trial, *because of* the way that I had answered questions that the authorities found unpleasant." If either of these two meanings is intended, the year 1986 (mentioned here) necessitates that the author would have had to have been put in the cell *after* the trial in which five years were added on to his term (because this better reflects the chronology given in his earlier memoir, *A Path Not Lined With Roses*, and various unpublished oral accounts).

and they were free to read it). I also told them that the path to freedom[139] must pass through repentance.

When we exited the cell, the officer accompanying us asked if we knew what kind of people we had just been talking to.

"Of course not," we answered.

"These are civil officials," he explained, "who have abused their power." (In other words, they were policemen, prosecutors, investigators, judges, etc.) Then it was clear to me why some of them had been so aggressively set against people in authority.

Then we entered a cell where there were three young, pregnant women. The oldest of them was about twenty-five. It was such a shame to look upon these people perverted by sin. After I had greeted them, I testified to them also of the great love and mercy of God, and about how they can be happy, if only they would repent of their sins and receive Jesus Christ into their hearts by faith as their personal Savior.

Of this consists true happiness. After I had bade them good health and a soon release, we departed this cell and set off toward the main corridor. My heart was sad from the suffering of unbelievers that I had seen. Such is reality without God, without His truth, without His light and love.

We parted company with the officer who had been accompanying us, and accompanied a journalist to the Directorate (UIN)[140] to see General Philippov, but he was not at his desk. While waiting for the general, we talked with his assistant in charge of the educational unit, Lt. Col. Korytin. He was interested in our impression of what we had seen. We spoke what was on our hearts. It goes without saying that we spoke to this man about the problem of sin, God, eternal life, and about how all of us must one day stand before God, to whom we will have to give an account of the life we have lived.

He did not resist our testimony in the least, and naturally, this was a good time of sowing God's Truth, both to this official, and to the young

---

[139] The word used for "freedom" here is actually the term "will," in the sense of, "the *freedom* to exercise one's will." This term is generally used only in legal proceedings, or in *prison* (which is understandable, since convicts would generally have a good grasp of technical legal language, having been tried in court and subjected to legal terminology in the cases against them). The significance is that the author is using "inside" terminology to present the Gospel in convict terms to convicts.

[140] The Directorate of Punishment and Corrections, as mentioned above.

lady journalist. We finally parted from these companions, having decided that we could no longer wait for the general, and made our way without haste toward the exit to the city.

A car passed us, then hit the brakes. General Philippov himself stepped out and waved for us to come back. We strode up to the general and thanked him for his service to us. We informed him that our visit had come to an end. The last thing we intended to see was the advocate who gave my defense in 1985–86.

The general expressed interest in our impressions during our visit to the prison and camps, and he wanted to know if anything had changed in those places compared to the time when I had been detained there as a criminal. We responded that, naturally, there had been huge changes.

As we parted company with the general, we wished him the very best for his family and his [military] service, and also that we might meet in the Lord's presence in Heaven. When we parted, I was left with a sort of pleasant feeling about how such a busy, important person had been simple and accessible to talk to us. Our Jesus died, of course, for General Philippov, too, and for all those who burn away their lives in these dark, dank cells...

In the early evening we contacted attorney Ludmila Aleksandrovna Belkina by telephone and agreed to meet. We met Ludmila Aleksandrovna at the appointed time in the courtyard of the building were she lives. The meeting was as if we were long-lost relatives.

I can say that this was a pleasant meeting. Some eighteen years earlier she, even though she was a Communist, understood as a human being that I was being accused under fabricated charges, and she bravely and honestly stood up to defend me. By defending me, she laid her career and her very life on the line to incur the disfavor of the KGB. Once, during one of the court's recesses, she was threatened that if she continued to defend me so earnestly, then she would be put on trial right along with me. She understood fully that these weren't the kind of people to joke around. All the same, she replied, "As I have defended him, so shall I continue his defense." This was a great risk on her part, since the whole case was a KGB fabrication.

Ludmila Aleksandrovna invited us into her home. After she kindly prepared tea, we heartily thanked the Lord in prayer for the mercies He sent through this woman. As we were drinking tea, Ludmila pulled a thick file from the shelf and said as she opened it, "These are my notes from your trial."

I was pleasantly surprised and asked if she might allow me to keep the file. With great joy and fanfare, she gave it to me. Then we reminisced about many things we had lived through, both pleasant and unpleasant episodes of that time. Ludmila related that the presiding judge in the case G.A. Simonova had retired, and that investigator N.M. Titova was now employed as a judge in the Chita Oblast regional court.[141]

I wanted to meet with these people and with Prosecutor Pogrebny and inform them that, on the basis of the Presidential Decree Concerning Amnesty, I had the right to bring criminal charges against them for fabricating a criminal case against me, and for the false and libelous sentence of five years of incarceration. However, we had already purchased return tickets. Of course, I do not hold any offense against them, or any desire to avenge their lawless acts. But I would like to testify to them while there is still time, while they are alive, that it is still possible for them to repent and accept Jesus Christ.

Before leaving Ludmila, I asked if she believed in God. She answered in the affirmative, and as she stood up to take a Bible from the shelf, she stated that she now reads this Book—though not as often as she might like. Before closing our meeting in prayer, we thanked Ludmila and expressed our desire to meet again: if not on earth, then in Heaven in eternity. She agreed.

After parting from Ludmila, we headed back to the apartment where we were staying. After tea, we warmly and heartily thanked Brother Vladimir and his wife for their hospitality and concern for us, and then set off for the train station.

In the train compartment we fell fast asleep and only woke up when some people walked through the car selling Omul fish. This fish lives

---

[141] Since an oblast is roughly equivalent to a state in the US, this position would be similar to being a State Supreme Court justice.

in Lake Baikal and is very tasty.[142] We bought some fish, and I told my son Pavel how I had dreamed in August 1985 (upon release from my five-year term) of making a stop in Baikal to eat this delicious fish. But they didn't release me then, and it took eighteen more years for my dream to be realized. What a shame that our trip didn't take place in the summer, when the beauty of the lake captivates every traveler!

Along the way, we enjoyed pleasant conversations with the other passengers. How unfortunate that our people know so little about the Gospel and are thus superstitious and caught up in witchcraft and sorcery![143] We made a stop at Perm station, since Chusovaya Station was on the way before us. On the morning of the next day, we were at the station we needed.

However, we didn't know how to find the last prison zone,[144] where I was sent from Chita. A policeman helped us by explaining how to find the bus station. At the bus station, the Lord sent us a woman who not only told us how to get to where we needed, but was going that same direction herself.

Finally, we arrived at the village of Kuchano, where one of the political zones—VS 389/36—was located. While we were still on the bus, we had been told that a museum had now been set up on the site of the prison. In reality, the awful prison no longer exists. Now in its place stands a memorial to the history of the political repressions of "Perm-36."[145]

We were greeted hospitably and, after getting acquainted with the administration of the Center, we got into a discussion with them. It turned out that one of the security guards at the museum had been a guard in the prison. I related how I had been transferred from Chita, how I had been kept for eleven days in an isolation chamber, how the administrators came every day to ask me how I was going to behave here: Would I openly pray

---

[142] Omul (*Coregonus autumnalis migratorius*) is a salmon-like fish found only in Lake Baikal, in Siberia. Smoked Omul is a highlight of the trans-Siberian Railway journey for many travelers, and caviar from the Omul is considered a delicacy.

[143] Although the author may be speaking figuratively here, the practice of literal witchcraft is quite widespread in Russia.

[144] I.e., prison colony.

[145] This area is internationally infamous for the atrocities committed under the Soviet regime.

and propagate faith in God? Would I work? I answered all their questions affirmatively. They didn't appreciate that sort of answer, and they promised to keep me in isolated punishment indefinitely, but without giving me bedding, shoes, or hat, leaving me only light worker's coveralls.

When I had asked them why they didn't place me in the general prison population, they answered that I had to go through quarantine after being in transit for such a long time. Of course, this was a lie. They were really just trying to break my will and to frighten me with the conditions in this terrible cell. When they finally transferred me into the general population, I was placed in Group № 1, where I worked assembling circuit boards for electric irons.

Back in the present, I asked the administration for permission to stroll around the former prison area and take a few photographs. The museum director gave permission, and we set off on an excursion through the museum.

We began our survey at the same cell where I spent those eleven days. Then they showed us a display with a model of the Perm-36 concentration camp itself, as well as displays of the GULAGs of Yakutia and Kalyma. Then we looked at the dilapidated barracks of Group № 1 where I had lived; but we decided not to go in, since this would have been life-threatening. We also visited the boiler room, where I had repaired the boilers. The boiler area held a lot of special memories for me. My memory was flooded with images of those distant days, when a KGB major who oversaw this prison decided to kill me in a terrible, cold cell because I openly prayed every day.

After morning prayer they had called me into the camp director's office and asked me, "Why did you pray today?"

"I always pray, and today I prayed the same as always."

Then the director put a protocol on the desk and asked me to look it over and sign it. The protocol read basically that, because I had prayed in the morning—openly—I would have to be placed in special segregation for thirty days. Naturally, I refused to sign, but two lieutenants were called in to sign for me. My heart sank at the thought of what lay in store for me, since I knew that even a single day in this cell could be terrible torment, even fatal. Outside, the temperature was already well below freezing, and there was no glass in the windows. So, the temperature was the same in the cell as it was outside.

They told me to leave the office, so I asked the officer, "Where do I go? To the cell?"

"Go back to your work group for now."

At work, I kept expecting them to come any minute to put me in the cell. They still had not taken me to the cell by lunch time, but when the order was given to go to lunch, I suddenly felt someone tug my shoulder. I turned to see an officer, who asked me to follow him. We went to some kind of room, and when I entered I saw the assistant warden sitting behind a desk with my personal file open before him.

When I greeted him, he responded, "Can you repair boilers for heating?"

"Yes, I can."

He was pleased with my response, and related how that morning and the night before two high-power boilers had broken down, and they were forced to switch to the two remaining medium-sized boilers. He added that if one more boiler broke down, "...not only will both we and soldiers freeze to death, but so will you."

The temperature outside was –45°, and the forecast was a further drop in temperature by nightfall. This administrator explained to me that he had looked over many personal files [of those in the camp], and he

This is a boiler that I repaired in January 1986. Thanks to this repair work, God redeemed me from the punishment cell.

had not found a single person who could repair boilers. Essentially, the prisoners here were politicians and journalists who knew how to work well with the pen.

He promised to give me one old man to help, and then said, "Go. Eat quickly, and get to work right away."

I didn't walk out, but rather flew as if on wings. I was thanking the Lord for the mercy He had shown me by

179

freeing me from this punishment cell and dismantling the terrible intentions of evil men.

For two weeks we repaired boilers, while I continued praying openly just like before. Now nobody bothered me. But as soon as the repair on the boilers was complete, that very same evening I was called before the administration, and the protocol was again presented, by which I was to be placed in segregation.

Then they softened their tone and said that this time they would not put me in the cell. They would just suspend my ability to get supplemental foodstuffs at the camp for a month, and they would take away my next scheduled opportunity to receive a package of food from home—which was scheduled two and a half years from then. Meanwhile, they threatened me again that if I would continue to pray openly, then they would certainly put me in this cell.

Of course, I continued to pray openly and never veered from this principle. Then, a week later, they summoned me into the administrative building after work and performed a search. They stripped me naked and looked through all my clothes and my shoes, all the while making a scene as if they were looking for something important.

I jokingly asked, "Wouldn't it be better for you to tell me what you're looking for, so I can just go ahead and bring it to you?"

My jesting suggestion sparked the most terrible threats ever directed at me.[146] All the same, God did not allow my persecutors to incarcerate me in that cell. Exactly one week later I was transferred to Perm Prison, where a high-ranking prosecutor[147] informed me that my case was being reviewed by Moscow and that I would be released soon. This is exactly what happened by the will of Almighty God in February 1987.

From the boiler room Pavel and I walked to the cafeteria, and on the way we were shown a display of various portraits. Above the photographs was written in large letters, "Executioners and Their Victims." Truly, there

---

146 The author gives no further details as to the exact content of these threats, though the reader will certainly be able to fill in the blank sufficiently, based on the character of those making the threats as recounted here.

147 The Russian term is actually more akin to the Roman office of "procurator," essentially, a District Attorney.

were the portraits of the biggest executioners in the Soviet Union, from Dzerzhinsky[148] to the last… Below them were photographs of wonderful people from Primorsky Krai who had been executed at various times. Among them was the photo of a simple nun who had been executed merely because she affirmed the existence of God.

In the cafeteria I sat at a table and reminisced about how the three of us[149] would stand and openly pray to ask the blessing on the food. This behavior incurred the wrath of the KGB men, and they really kept us in their sights.

Next Pavel and I got our picture taken with the administrator of the museum, and with the former guard, for whom I hold no animosity. Then we bade farewell and set off for Chusovaya Station. Pavel and I rode by bus, and I remembered those days when I was transported on this road in a "Black Maria"—as a rule, always at night.

But Pavel imagined a different picture: how he and his mother (my wife) had traveled this road to visit me in prison. The bus had been so cold that it was simply not possible to warm one's feet. The prison administration did not allow the visit to take place then, so Pavel had to ride back with legs and feet half-frozen, with his heart full of pain from the visit that never was. But our God gave us the strength to endure all through the might of Jesus Christ, who loves us.

From Chusovaya Station we successfully rode to Perm. The trip back to Moscow was quite pleasant. There were two young women with us in the train compartment all the way back to Moscow, and we had nice conversations about God, eternal life, about good and holy living on earth. As we bade farewell to these women, we expressed our wish to one day meet again: next time in that world hereafter, in God's paradise, if they would accept Christ into their hearts and repent of their sins.

And so, filled with satisfaction over various encounters, we successfully returned home. Our God in a miraculous way kept us safe on the journey.

To Him be praise for the ages of the ages! Amen.

---

[148] Felix Dzerzhinsky was the founder of the Secret Police under Vladimir Lenin, the organization that eventually became the KGB.

[149] It is unclear from the narrative to whom "the three of us" refers, precisely.

APPENDIX I:
Russian Songs Referred to in the Text

I Have Sinned, Oh My Lord, Before Thee

I have sinned, Oh My Lord, before Thee.
You see the evil in my doings,
You see the sin of my soul enshrouded in shadow.
Look Thou upon the torment in mine eyes!
The din of my groaning is not hidden before Thee,
The flood of my tears is great,
How long shall I be tortured, broken?
How long shalt Thou be from me estranged?
Deal Thou not with me according to my sins,
And repay me not by reason of my guilt.
With a troubed soul I am searching for Thee,
Reveal Thy clear countenance unto me.
Fill up my soul early with grace,
My God, and Father and Liege!
Give the saving and longed-for salvation,
For Thou alone can'st give it.
Oh help Thou my inconstant feet
To find again Thy path,
That I may serve my God anew,
As a son and humble servant.
Hear Thou the tormented sounds of this supplication,
And come Thou Thyself unto mine aid!
Guide me as a prodigal son
By the hand unto salvation.

My Path Like the Others' Is Not Lined With Flowers

My path like the others' is not lined with flowers
Fragrant roses do not grow there
My path is covered all over with thorns,
And gnarled thistles are the only thing growing there.

I walk on, my legs fiercely wounded
And the path before me seems hard.
But a voice from somewhere far off in my soul
Confidently whispers, "Fear not. Go on."

That voice the Savior does plant in my soul
And he gives me the strength for my battle with sin.
He promises to give me a heavenly kingdom:
Love and blessedness forever with Christ.

Now this path, it seems to me, is not so hard,
And joy has been poured into my heart and fills it.
Behold, I am approaching the blessed gates
Where there is happiness eternal and the lights of eternal days.

Now that voice from heaven is inviting me:
"Oh weary and tormented wayfarer of the earth,
A holy reward awaits you,
Come, now, more quickly into heavenly glory.

God, God, Give Me The Strength to Lay My Life Down for My Neighbors

God, God, give me the strength
To lay my life down for my neighbors,
And to my heart unto the grave [give strength]
To forgive all offenses of my enemies.

Don't let me make peace with the lie
In this cold life war,
And teach me to pray,
To pray fervently to You.

Let them throw stones at my chest,
Not knowing the sentiments of saints,
Let them hate me, curse me, —
I will lay down my life for them.

Oh, Lord, in the words of cursing
Yea, all on this earth shall revile me,
But I will open to them my embrace,
Keeping the commandment of Christ.

Oh, give me strength in my suffering soul
All of Your covenants to keep,
And help me the slander of mine enemies
In meekness to bear.

What Awaits Me, I Know Not

What awaits me, I know not,
My Lord has hidden this,
But firmly I am certain:
He's laid out my path before Me,
Fullness of Life, goodness and strength
In His love He has revealed.

Chorus:
Wherever my Lord calls
There doth His child haste.
"He knows the path, He knows!"
[The child] trustingly affirms.

All around is in eclipse,
With labor, I go forward.
But in God there is enlightenment,
He Himself doth lead me
And often on His shoulders bears me
In time of storm and unhappiness.

Among trial and misfortune
May my flesh keep silent.
But among the silence
May a voice come clearly through:
"You are Mine! Your path is in My hand,
Fear not troubled days!"

So I go on not knowing,
Nor seeking e'en to know
What will be, I only want
To give the Lord my path,
How sweet to walk with Him [even] in the darkness,
And to live without Him is to wander.

APPENDIX II:
Selected Articles from the Soviet Constitution

Because many of the events as related in this book occurred in a country whose political and legal traditions are far different from those of the readers, we thought it might be helpful to include selections form the Constitution of the USSR. It is our hope that this will dispel some possible misconceptions concerning Soviet law and be an informative aid to the reader.

At first glance, many are surprised at the democratic-sounding provisions of the Soviet Constitution, which is a characteristic that even survived the twenty-year re-write under Brezhnev. As one observer put it, however, "The Soviet Constitution of 1936 'listed an impressive array of individual and political rights, yet no Soviet citizen in his right mind would have thought of invoking them." [150] *Even from a purely social standpoint, the Rumachik story is compelling precisely because they dared to invoke those rights.*

Above all, we have chosen these portions of the Soviet Constitution to demonstrate that the Rumachiks were persecuted for activities that are explicitly guaranteed as their rights under Soviet law, and that this same law explicitly forbids the persecution of which this book tells the account.

A. SELECTIONS FROM THE 1936 CONSTITUTION OF THE USSR

ARTICLE 124. In order to ensure to citizens freedom of conscience, the church in the USSR is separated from the state, and the school from the church. <u>Freedom of religious worship and freedom of anti-religious propaganda is recognized for all citizens.</u>

ARTICLE 125. In conformity with the interests of the working people, and in order to strengthen the socialist system, the citizens of the USSR are <u>guaranteed by law</u>: a. <u>freedom of speech</u>; b. <u>freedom of the press</u>; c.

---

[150] Ulam, A. *Russia's Failed Revolutions.* New York: Basic Books, Inc. 1981. p. 421, as quoted by Tania E. Lozansky in her paper "The Role of Dissent in the Soviet Union since 1953." *The Concord Review.* 1996, date of authorship: 1989

186

freedom of assembly, including the holding of mass meetings; d. freedom of street processions and demonstrations.
These civil rights are ensured by placing at the disposal of the working people and their organizations printing presses, stocks of paper, public buildings, the streets, communications facilities and other material requisites for the exercise of these rights.

ARTICLE 126. In conformity with the interests of the working people, and in order to develop the organizational initiative and political activity of the masses of the people, citizens of the USSR are ensured the right to unite in public organizations—trade unions, cooperative associations, youth organizations,' sport and defense organizations, cultural, technical and scientific societies; and the most active and politically most conscious citizens in the ranks of the working class and other sections of the working people unite in the Communist Party of the Soviet Union (Bolsheviks), which is the vanguard of the working people in their struggle to strengthen and develop the socialist system and is the leading core of all organizations of the working people, both public and state.

ARTICLE 127. Citizens of the USSR are guaranteed inviolability of the person. No person may be placed under arrest except by decision of a court or with the sanction of a procurator.

ARTICLE 128. The inviolability of the homes of citizens and privacy of correspondence are protected by law.

B. SELECTIONS FROM THE 1977 CONSTITUTION OF THE USSR

Article 34. Citizens of the USSR are equal before the law, without distinction of origin, social or property status, race or nationality, sex, education, language, attitude to religion, type and nature of occupation, domicile, or other status. The equal rights of citizens of the USSR are guaranteed in all fields of economic, political, social, and cultural life.

Article 49. Every citizen of the USSR has the right to submit proposals to state bodies and public organizations for improving their activity, and to criticize shortcomings in their work. Officials are obliged, within established time limits, to examine citizens' proposals and requests, to reply to them, and to take appropriate action.

Persecution for criticism is prohibited. Persons guilty of such persecution shall be called to account.

Article 50. In accordance with the interests of the people and in order to strengthen and develop the socialist system, citizens of the USSR are guaranteed freedom of speech, of the press, and of assembly, meetings, street processions and demonstrations.

Exercise of these political freedoms is ensured by putting public buildings, streets and squares at the disposal of the working people and their organizations, by broad dissemination of information, and by the opportunity to use the press, television, and radio.

Notice here the subtle changes in verbiage between Article 125 of the 1936 Constitution and this article. The words "by law" and "mass meetings" have been omitted.

Article 51. In accordance with the aims of building communism, citizens of the USSR have the right to associate in public organizations that promote their political activity and initiative and satisfaction of their various interests.

Public organizations are guaranteed conditions for successfully performing the functions defined in their rules.

Article 52. Citizens of the USSR are guaranteed freedom of conscience, that is, the right to profess or not to profess any religion, and to conduct religious worship or atheistic propaganda. Incitement of hostility or hatred on religious grounds is prohibited.

In the USSR, the church is separated from the state, and the school from the church.

This article served as the legal basis for establishing the "League of Militant Atheists," as its name implies, a group openly hostile to Christianity.

Article 53. <u>The family enjoys the protection of the state</u>.
Marriage is based on the free consent of the woman and the man; spouses are completely equal in their family relations.
The state helps the family by providing and developing a broad system of childcare institutions, by organizing and improving communal services and public catering, by paying grants on the birth of a child, by providing children's allowances and benefits for large families, and other forms of family allowances and assistance.

This article along with Article 66 provides a constitutional defense for the removal of children from their parents' custody.

Article 54. <u>Citizens of the USSR are guaranteed inviolability of the person</u>. No one may be arrested except by a court decision or on the warrant of a procurator.

Article 55. <u>Citizens of the USSR are guaranteed inviolability of the home</u>. No one may, without lawful grounds, enter a home against the will of those residing in it.

Article 56. <u>The privacy of citizens, and of their correspondence, telephone conversations, and telegraphic communications is protected by law.</u>

Article 57. <u>Respect for the individual and protection of the rights and freedoms of citizens</u> are the duty of all state bodies, public organizations, and officials. Citizens of the USSR have the right to protection by the courts against encroachments on their honor and reputation, life and health, and personal freedom and property.

Article 58. <u>Citizens of the USSR have the right to lodge a complaint against the actions of officials, state bodies and public bodies</u>. Complaints shall be examined according to the procedure and within the time limit established by law.
<u>Actions by officials that contravene the law or exceed their powers, and infringe the rights of citizens, may be appealed in a court in the manner prescribed by law.</u>

Citizens of the USSR have the right to compensation for damage resulting from unlawful actions by state organizations and public organizations, or by officials in the performance of their duties.

Article 66. Citizens of the USSR are obliged to concern themselves with the upbringing of children, to train them for socially useful work, and to raise them as worthy members of socialist society. Children are obliged to care for their parents and help them.

NOTE: *We have added highlights to those sections of the text that we felt were the most grossly violated by the actions of the Soviet government as related in this text. It bears noting, however, that the articles enumerated here are not the only ones to have been violated by the Soviet government during its tenure. Though many studies on this subject have been published, there is to our knowledge no exhaustive work on the subject of the atrocities committed by the Soviet regime.*

APPENDIX III:
Search Warrant

The following search warrant lists the kinds of items taken during the searches discussed in this account. It is worth noting that several of the items confiscated appear to have little relevance—if any—to the apparent investigation.

Search Protocol

City of Dyedovsk
7 February 1980

I, Investigator for the Istra City Prosecutor's Office, V.I. Dimitrieva, in the presence of witnesses Fedosov, Nikolai Alekseevich; Ilasin, Alexander Anatolyevich; and in the presence of the municipal inspector for the Dyedovsk State Police Department (GOM) Zamorinkov, arrived in the city of Dyedovsk for the purpose of conducting a search in the apartment of one Rumachik, Lubov Vasilievna, residing in the city of Dyedovsk at the following address: ul. Bolnichnaya d. 13 kv. 51, for the purpose of carrying out a search in compliance with the warrant to that effect issued on 6 February 1980 by Investigator for the Office of the Prosecutor, MSSR,[151] Tsurkan.

Upon requesting that she open the door, Rumachik, L.V. did not open it. After having called the Superintendent Director of the Industrial Union of Technical Fabrics, Ludmila Borisovna Solovyova and the Deputy of the Dyedovsk City Soviet,[152] Maria Ivanovna Yegereva, L.V. Rumachik was advised that the door would be broken in if she did not open it willingly. When they began to break the lock, L.V. Rumachik opened the door.

This act has been established in the presence of L.V. Rumachik and M.P. Rumachik.

---

[151] MSSR: Moldavian Soviet Socialist Republic

[152] Soviet: or, "City Council." The Soviet Union was so named because the political system was based on hierarchically structured "councils" (in Russian, soviet).

7 February 1980

[signed]
Inspector Dimitrieva

[signed]   [signed]
Deputy Yegereva   Witness Fedosova

[signed]   [signed]
Superintendent Director Solovyeva   Ilasin

Following is an enumerated list of items confiscated during the aforementioned search, the page listing items 1–24 is missing:

25. Brochure: "A Christian Outline for the Christian Minister" Printed on a manual type machine and bound by hand. 1 copy.
26. Brochure: "The True Christian" Author: Theologian G. Kh. Weis. Publisher: "Christian Press."[153] 1 copy.
27. Brochure: "Much Prayer – Much Power" Author: Peter Deyneka. Chicago, USA, Publisher: Slavic Gospel Society. Prepared by photocopy. 1 copy.
28. Brochure: "The Greatest Love in the World" Author: Henry Drummand. 1 copy
29. Bible. In German. Published 1969. Berlin. 1 copy
30. Brochure: "About God–The Holy Spirit" Prepared by photocopy. 1 copy
31. Brochure: "Notes for Studying the Gospel of John" Author: V.F. Martsinkovski. 1 copy
32. Copy of trial documents from 11 May 1967 pertaining to Zakayev et. al. 5 pages, written in manuscript text.
33. Journal: "Messenger of Salvation #3, 1973"[154] 2 copies.

---

[153] This is the underground press founded in part by Peter Rumachik, and upon which we worked in conjunction with other believers.

[154] "Messenger of Salvation": This journal was the regular publication of the Committee of Prisoners' Relatives upon which Luba Rumachik worked, and which was established for the purpose of making known the plight of religious prisoners in the Soviet Union.

34. "Brotherly Leaflet #4"[155] 1973. 15 copies.
35. Bible. In Polish. Published 1922, Warsaw. 1 copy.
36. Book in Polish. Published: 1916, Riga. 1 copy.
37. Testament. Publisher "Christian Press." Pocket-size. 2 copies.
38. Brochure: "Memorandum from the Org-Committee Concerning the Congregation of the Evangelical Christian Baptists, 15-18 October." 1963. Printed by typewriter. 1 copy.
39. Texts of prayers and appeals to believers. 6 pages. Prepared by photocopy.
40. Illustrated Publication: "The Life of Christ." Made in Sweden. 1 copy.
41. Postcards, with text on reverse side. 6 pcs.
42. "Manual for the Congregation of Evangelical Christian Baptists." Typewritten, 56 pages. 5 copies.
43. "Manual for Preaching." Typewritten, 101 pages. 1 copy.
44. "Advice for the Ordination of Ministers." Typewritten. 2 pages. 1 copy.
45. "An Open Letter to Believers of the Evangelical Christian Baptists from Member of the Moscow Church of Evangelical Christian Baptists A.S. Elkanda." Typewritten. 2 pages. 16 copies.
46. "An Appeal to the Council of Churches, ECB, to All Christian Baptists." Printed on a mass-copy machine. 12 pages. 1 copy.
47. Article: "Life Consecrated to a Higher Purpose." Typewritten. 35 pages. 1 copy.
48. "Brotherly Leaflet." #4, 1973. 1 copy
   #2, 1973. 1 copy
   #1, 1973, 1 copy
   #5, 1972, 1 copy
49. Addresses from USA, Santa Ana
   [sic.] from Vinitskaya Oblast. Tvenduk and Gursogova. 2 pages.
50. Brochure: "Christian Youth." Published 1973. Typewritten. 3 copies.
51. Photographs: Memorial [or birthday] revelers, in church, ECB. 1 page. 1 copy.

---

[155] "Brotherly Leaflet": Another publication of the Committee of Prisoners' Relatives.

All items found during the search as indicated in points 1–11 were confiscated by the investigator. During the search, P.V. Rumachik did indicate that in accordance with the particulars of the warrant concerning what literature was to be confiscated, that it was thereby forbidden to take religious literature; moreover, he protested the taking of pictures as the search was being conducted; moreover, he protested the confiscation of personal monies.

No other complaints or concerns were indicated.

This protocol has been duly read and written correctly.[156]

Signature of the person being searched: _____
[not signed]

Witnesses' signatures: [signatures]

Investigator: [signature][157]

Copy of this protocol received by: _____
[not signed]

Rumachik protests that they have not been left 100 rubles to feed the family.[158]
Rumachik has refused to sign this document.

Investigator [signature]   Witnesses [signatures]

---

[156] That is, the person preparing this report attests on her own recognaissance that the report is correct without any corroborating testimony to that effect.

[157] The signature of the investigator listed here does not match the name of the investigator as indicated earlier in this document.

[158] That is, since all the funds found were confiscated, Peter Rumachik has indicated that they are not left with any money to buy food.

Items Confiscated in Other Searches

1974
4. Personal Bibles, 5 copies. Brochure
9. Calendar for the year 1974. With captions: "The Lord is near," "Time to seek the Lord" on page 6. [8 calendars?][159]
10. Bulletin of the Council of Prisoners' Relatives. #12. 3 October 1973.
17. Money in the sum of 5,300 rubles in a plastic bag imprinted with the embossing "NTO."[160]
24. Christian Stories for Children. Translated from English. Photocopy.

1983
5. Bookshelf[161]
8. Season's greetings card: "Happy New Year!"[162]
11. Newspaper in a foreign language.[163]
12. Reed pipe, with the inscription "Concerning our hope"[164]

---

[159] In one account, Pastor Rumachik related that at the trial, this calendar was used as evidence of anti-Soviet activity. The prosecution maintained that the clocks shown as part of the motif in the picture for this month showed by the positioning of their hands the exact time that the Christians planned to overthrow the Soviet Union.

[160] Approximately the equivalent of $6,600, though Soviet state controlled currency values at the time make it hard to determine the actual value.

[161] Several of the items selected from the list of confiscated items appear to have no relative bearing on the investigation, as in the example here of why the prosecution would deem it necessary to take a bookshelf when the warrant presumably calls for the confiscation of "seditious" literature.

[162] There is no indication on this list that this card even contains any religious content. The New Year holiday was also held as an official Communist observance, since it has no overtly religious meaning associated with it as in the cases of Christmas and Easter.

[163] Again, there is no indication that the contents of this paper are in any way anti-Soviet or seditious. It was apparently confiscated for the mere fact that it was written in a foreign language. Evidence of this kind was often used to portray Christians as spies.

[164] The word translated here as "hope" is the word "trust" found in Psalm 7:1 as well as other places in Scripture. While this particular word has definite religious overtones (eg. It "sounds" Biblical), there is little support for the argument that this is a decidedly religious inscription, and certainly not an anti-Soviet one.

15. Handwritten poems.[165]
23. Selected Works.[166]

1980
11. Trial documents for Mosevitski.

1983
2. Questionnaire form.[167]
4. Letter addressed to L.P. Rumachik from Kishinevskaya Oblast[168] from M.V. Tkachuk.

---

[165] The documents give no indication as to the nature of these poems, whether they are anti-Soviet, religious, or otherwise.

[166] The author is not indicated. These could be the selected works of anyone.

[167] Apparently, an official form. Nothing here indicates this item to be anti-Soviet or religious.

[168] In Moldava, one of the republics of the Soviet Union, located southwest of Ukraine.

APPENDIX IV:
Expert Testimony Used Against Peter V. Rumachik

The following is expert testimony used in one of the trials against Brother Rumachik. Here we see clearly the way in which the Soviet authorities manipulated evidence to make it appear that Christians were actively warring against the Soviet regime in an effort to overthrow it.

INCARCERATION

Expert testimony for the criminal trial to be used in accusation of Rumachik, Peter Vasilyevich in accordance with Art. 142, subsec. II of the Criminal Codex of the RSFSR[169]

By issue of the Investigator for the Prosecution for the City of Istra O.V. Kuznetsov for a scientific expert analysis of the contents and affiliation of the religious literature confiscated from Rumachik, P.V. for the carrying out of this expert analysis, Candidate of Philosophical Sciences F. I. Grakavenko[170] was assigned the task of explaining the following questions:

1. What is the affiliation and overall direction of the literature presented to the expert witness?
2. Do the contents of the confiscated literature indicate any of the internal problems of the church?
3. Is there contained in the given literature any reason or reason by implication for the non-fulfillment of Soviet legislation concerning religious cults?

---

[169] The statute in question is as follows: **Violation of Laws on Separation of Church and State and of Church and School.** *The violation of laws on the separation of church and state and of school and church shall be ounished by correctional tasks for a term not exceeding one year or by a fine not exceeding 50 rubles.* The same acts committed by a person previously convicted of violation of laws on the separation of church and state and of school and church, as well as organizational activity directed toward the commission of such acts, shall be punished by deprivation of freedom for a term not to exceed three years.

[170] Candidate of Philosophical Sciences: This is a considerably esteemed position of learning in the USSR. In the U.S., this would be something similar to a Ph.D., with the exception that a degree of this kind is more rare in Russia than in the U.S.

Concerning the rights and responsibilities of the expert council in accor-dance with article 82 of the Criminal Codex of the Russian Soviet Federated Socialist Republic and of his responsibility of refusal or absti-nence of submitting the prisoner to false imprisonment or [of submitting evidence] leading to [false imprisonment] the expert has been advised.[171]

In accordance with the task set forth by the investigator for expert analysis, the following materials are presented [as exhibits for evidence]

1. "Brotherly Leaflet," organ of the Council of Churches, ECB, 1969, #7-8
2. Brochure: "Foundations of the Position of Our Brotherhood." (Handwritten)
3. Folio: Begins with the words: "I have given you an example…"
4. Folio: "Dispute with a Professor of Astronomy."
5. Paper with question listed of a religious nature.
6. Paper with question listed of a religious nature.
7. Poem: "Listen, oh, friend"[172]
8. Sheet of paper with the heading: "The greatest intelligent question," "Prepare for this event."
9. Letter concerning the sin of Brother Prokofiev
10. Hymnal of religious songs.
11. Song: "Mother Cried Beside Her Bed."
12. "Messenger of Salvation," 1969. #2.

---

[171] The first half of Article 82 of the RSFSR Code of Criminal Procedure enumerates the expert witness' right to evidence and to interrogate witnesses in connection with his part of the investigation. This Article Also stipulates, "An expert shall be obliged to apear when summoned by a person [or court] conducting an inquiry…In the event that an expert refuses to fulfill or evades fulfilling his duties without valid reasons, or gives an opinion known to be false, or fails to appear without valid reasons when summoned by a person conducting an inquiry…the measures provided by Article 73 of the present code shall be applied." Said measures in this case would subject the witness to up to six months' incarceration, a fine of 50 rubles or social censure in the event that he refused to give testimony, or up to one year incarceration if said testimony was false.

[172] The word "friend" is not capitalized in this document. In Russian, as in English, divine names and titles are capitalized. Communist literature and documents made a point of omitting the capitalization of the words: "god," "lord," etc.

13. Proclamation:[173] "Depart from me, ye who work iniquity."
14. Folio: "In works that violate the will of God…"
15. Letter: "Protest" – addressed to N.S. Krushchev from 3 May 1962 (manuscript)[174]
16. "Declaration" addressed to N.S. Khrushchev from 28 June 1962. (Manuscript)
17. Letter addressed to N.S. Khrushchev. February 1963. (Typewritten)
18. Letter addressed to N.S. Khrushchev. November 1962. (Typewritten)
19. Proclamation: "The Sending of the Church of God." (Hectograph)
20. Proclamation:[175] "An Epistle to the Presidium from the AU-ECB in the USSR." (Hectograph)
21. Proclamation: "Christmas"[176]
22. Proclamation: "An Amazing Message," from 2 August 1968 (typewritten)
23. Proclamation: "To All Christian Believers Residing in the Territory of the USSR," from 6 August 1968. (Hectograph)
24. Proclamation: " An Amazing Message," from 15 May 1968

---

[173] Proclamation: It is of essential importance in understanding this document to note what the prosecution has done in choosing this word. The "proclamations" (*proklamatsii*) listed here are obviously *sermon notes*. The word *propoved* is most correctly understood as "sermon" or "homily," though it may also mean a "political speech." By calling these sermons "proclamations," the witness has turned them into political propaganda rather than homilies. This tendency of re-interpreting the obvious meaning of the evidence to fit the intent of the prosecution will become more evident throughout the document.

[174] The reader should note two important points here: First, that Soviet law provides for the petitioning of the government to redress injustice, as is the case with this letter; and secondly, while the prosecution could have chosen to use these letters of protest to build a case for political agitation, they chose not to do so. Even though the letters are listed here, they are not used in the actual testimony.

[175] It seems apparent that the expert witness has mistakenly identified as a "proclamation" what actually appears to be a letter written to the Presidium of the USSR. NOTE: AC-ECB, "The All-Union [Council of] Evangelical Christian Baptists"

[176] The title of this "proclamation" makes it all the more evident that most of these supposed political proclamations are obviously sermons.

The study of this literature taken for use by the expert council is laid out in the following way:

1. Its general characteristics and a determination of its religious affiliation.
2. Research of the documents giving testimony to the war against Soviet laws concerning religious cults.
3. Research of the documents giving testimony to the activities directed toward the establishment and administration of children's schools, groups and study circles.

As the entire text of the deposition is too long to be included here, we have selected those parts of the remaining text that most directly contribute to the trial proceedings.

I.   The General Characteristics and Religious Affiliation of the Literature Presented for Expert Analysis.

In sub-points 1 and 2,the expert council establishes that Pastor Rumachik is affiliated with the STs-EKhB (Council of Churches of Evangelical Christian Baptists), a group that is not part of the officially recognized Baptist Church in the Soviet Union. This makes it distinct from the VSEKhB (All -Union Council [of Churches] of Evangelical Christian Baptists), which is the group that cooperated with the Soviet authorities.

4. The materials selected as the object of this study present in themselves...by the manner of their printing the purpose of mass distribution. The literature presented for expert analysis, by reason of its preparation (hectographic copying) and by designation is propagandist proclamatory literature, obviously intended for mass readership. Of this there is testimony in the fact that the literature contains the direct call for the reader to duplicate and by all means possible distribute it. The mass circulation of documents calling for the non-fulfillment of the legislation concerning religious cults is, by its very nature, nothing

more than an organized incitement to a significant number of persons to break the law.[177] The distribution of documents calling for non-fulfillment of legislation concerning religious cults is one of the primary elements of this organized activity.[178] It is essential to note that the very leaders of the Council of Churches, ECB are aware of this themselves. In one of the "appeals" of the STs-ECB to believers, the following is stated: "Those who have received sentences and chains for the sake of the written word[179] have become martyrs for the truth, suffering for the spreading[180] of gospel truths."

...On the basis of this "Appeal," "Epistle," "Exhortation," "Accounts," etc, we shall see how the official materials of the Council of Churches...[has] organized a war against the Soviet legislation concerning religious cults.

In the materials studied, the leaders of the Council accuse the All-Union Council leaders of "unlawfully joining with the powers of this world," "a corrupt union with the world," "unification with government authority." "The Church has made itself subject to worldly authority...In cunning fashion, satan and the world have pushed the church into the Pergamos period...[181] Something similar happened with us in the 1920's when satan began little by little to bring the brethren in charge under his subjection and through them to influence the church...The church became subject to the establishments of men...it turned out to be in a weakened state...In our day,

---

[177] According to the Soviet Constitution, distributing literature is perfectly legal. See: Appendix: SELECTED ARTICLES FROM THE 1936 CONSTITUTION OF THE USSR, Article 125.

[178] In other words, the Baptist movement in Russia is treated as "organized crime."

[179] That is, "the written Word," which is surely capitalized in the original source being quoted, though it is not so recorded here.

[180] Another possible translation here is "distribution" or "circulation," as this word is so translated elsewhere in the text.

[181] The reference here is to Revelation 2:12–17. Pergamos is described in this passage as the "seat of Satan"; many scholars believe that this is in reference to the cult of emperor worship prevalent there, which could be seen as a correlation to the human-centered Soviet Union. The church is accused in verse 14: "But I have a few things against thee, because thou hast there them that hold the doctrine of Balaam, who taught Balac to cast a stumblingblock before the children of Israel, to eat things sacrificed unto idols, and to commit fornication." In other words, the church is accused of compromise with the world.

satan dictates through the ministers of the All-Union Council,[182] and the church accepts all sorts of proposals that clearly go against god's commands, in which fashion the church reaches dissolution." (Por. V 19) Judging, then, from the relationship between the Soviet government and the All-Union Council, the believers are attempting, by painting the Soviet government in the form of "satan," to destroy our government and Soviet society.

In the official publications of the Council of Churches, ECB: "Brotherly Leaflet" and "Messenger of Salvation," as it is also underscored in the many proclamations, that the organizational committee of the Council of Churches, ECB battles against "the union of the church with the world," by which is understood, Soviet society. Stated differently, the goal of this war being carried out on the part of those who side with the Council of Churches, ECB, is anti-societal. To that end, the partisans of the Council of Churches, ECB, are organizing an active underground war against Soviet law, and in such fashion activities against society.

II.   The War Against Soviet Laws Concerning Religious Cults.

The materials given for analysis to the expert council allow the establishment of the clear representation of the goals and tasks of that *non-religious war* that is being conducted by the proponents of the Council of Churches, ECB. The clear formation of such an account (despite the attempts on their part to conceal and to mask the true goals of their war behind the defense that they are doing the works of Christ as they speak of the supposed…injustice of Soviet law) is to be found in the article, "To the Aid of the Lord with the Brave," published in the "Messenger of Salvation" (# 1 from 1965) and distributed in the form of individual leaflets to the Istra congregation of the ECB, of whom former Secretary of the Council of Churches, ECB, P.V. Rumachik is an active member…In this article, testimony is made to the fact that the initiative of this war proceeds from the leaders of the Council of Churches, ECB, among whom it is clear that until his trial P.V. Rumachik occupied a clear position, and not from the higher organs of the government and the Party,

---

[182] During Soviet times, there were even accounts that the KGB was able to install its agents as pastors in some of these churches!

as the proponents of the CC-ECB affirm in their documents, prepared as a lie to the rationale of the believers, where it says,[183]

"All who belong to the people of god must join in the fray[184] with Him. The war has been declared against uncleaness and all the enemies of god who have raised their hand against god's holiness. Every one of god's people has holy obligations: he must battle with all against the enemies of Emmanuel (Christ)…

Therefore, the battle involves all, not just selected congregations, groups, or gatherings—but all the people of God must rise up against the enemy…Very many believers think that god will do everything on His own…This is a great waywardness. You must certainly be His warrior…[185] You will be accursed if you don't repent of your [lack of] faithfulness and join the ranks of the brave warriors of God. Awaken from your dream and put on the full armor of God[186] and go with Him into the fray. Jesus, our king, will be the victor…

Cursed is he who thinks of himself while doing the work of God carelessly… In purity of heart, in oneness of spirit and with solid faith we will conduct God's war!

All are on call for God: young and old, men and women, strong and weak!

Onward to God's aid with the brave!

All of the given exhortations listed here have as their goal to organize a religious war against the "unfaithful" and the "enemies of Christ."

---

[183] It is interesting to note that, in condemning the accused, the expert witness dedicates at least a full page of the deposition to copying down a large portion of one of the texts confiscated as "anti-Soviet propaganda." Since this deposition was later given back to the prisoner for his records, there is no small irony in the fact that the very documentation given to the prisoner by the prosecution contained that very text that was most offensive to the government and which they did not want him to have in the first place.

[184] Fray: This is the word "battle" as it appears in many places in the Russian Synodal Translation of the Scriptures. (Compare 1 Samuel 17:20, 28) It should be clear that, because the word chosen to denote "battle" is a Scriptural term not generally found in common parlance, the battle implied is spiritual, not physical.

[185] This is a Scriptural term for "warrior" as found, for example, in 2 Timothy 2:3. Compare KJV "soldier."

[186] In the Russian Synodal text, this reads "put on the full armament…" which could be construed as a call to using modern weaponry.

In order to organize and provoke the ranks of believers into this war[187] against the "enemies of the work of God," the proponents of the CC-ECB use, above all, the false accusation[188] against the higher organs of the Soviet government and the Party, as if in the USSR believers are persecuted only for their religiousness (por. #15), as if the program established by the CPSU[189] is one of physical elimination believers (por. #1, 22, 24), as if the CPSU and the Soviet government meddle in the internal affairs of the ECB with the goal of eliminating it. (por #22, 24) There is contained in the literature given for analysis to the expert council a whole series of false accusations directed toward the higher organs of the Party and the government, having as their goal the provocation of a war against the enemies "of God," and along with this a war against the laws by stating the following sorts of activities are being carried out: 1) the use of the AU-ECB as a "State Church" of the USSR; 2) the organization of mass, centralized persecutions and repressions in relation to the believers in the USSR; 3) persecutions and repressions against the Baptists supposedly for their religious conviction, for their faith; 4) the liquidation of freedom of conscience in the USSR; 5) the conducting of genocide for political purposes, that is, the physical elimination of believers in the USSR; and 6) the conducting of "an administrative-physical war for the annihilation of religion and the church. These false accusations are in clear fashion directed toward rousing the believers against the organs of power, moving them to protest against the supposed injustice of Soviet legislation concerning religious cults. In this the organizers of this war, as seen in the materials found in the possession of P.V. Rumachik, do not stop at this heinous slander against our society, which [slander] has as its goal to the extent of all boundaries to anger the believers so as to bring them to war against those laws which limit the

---

[187] Article 71 of the RSFSR Criminal Codex prescribes "deprivation of freedom for a term of three to eight years, with or without additional exile to a term of two to five years" for "propagandizing of war."

[188] Under Article 70 of the RSFSR Criminal Codex, the crime of slander against the Soviet Union is punishable by "deprivation of freedom for a term of six months to seven years, with or without additional exile for a term of two to five years, or by exile to a term of two to five years."

[189] Or KPSS (Kommunistichestkaya Partiya Sovietskogo Soyuza): The Communist Party of the Soviet Union

religious extremists which head the Council of Churches, ECB.[190]

…Thus, in the literature confiscated from Citizen [Rumachik] the proclamation[191] entitled "Dear Children of God" speaks without reciprocity: "In order to be that same church of the first apostles, we must live in the Roman Empire. We have the joy of living in such an empire." (por. #12) Planting a question in this way clearly orients believers in a contrary position toward the legislation concerning religious cults. Of course, it is hard to imagine that the authors of this rousing affirmation do not know that in our country there has never been, nor can there be the question of forbidding belief in god or of boiling believers in cauldrons, etc. Yet at the same time they talk of such perspectives awaiting believers in the USSR. All of this has the conscious preemptive goal directed by the leadership of the CC-ECB defined as the psychological preparation of a specific mass of believers to voluntary suffering connected to that war against Soviet laws…

In the proclamation, "An Extraordinary Message" (por #24) a direct demand is put forth for alteration of Soviet laws. In this demand, attention is called [to the argument] that the proponents of the CC-ECB suffer not because of their faith, but because of their violation of Soviet laws:

The whole reason for these sufferings of the church in our land are contained in the sharp contradiction and non-conformity to the legislation concerning cults…to fundamental human rights…."

[In another "proclamation" found in the literature confiscated from P.V. Rumachik, the following was found:]

"Soviet legislation forbids the following:

1. Preaching the gospel (outside a church building).
2. Missionary activity.
3. Collectively bringing up children in the teaching of Christ.
4. Ecclesiastic good-will. (Charitable work).

---

[190] In other words, the whole gist of this text is to say that the Soviet government didn't really repress or eliminate anyone for their faith, and the laws were not designed for this purpose, even though they were designed to limit the activities of the "religious extremists" heading the underground Church. Which is the same as saying, "Soviet laws don't repress any religious people. They only repress this certain group of religious people."

[191] *sermon*

5. Acceptance into the church of people younger than 18 years of age.
6. Drawing believers away form social norms..."
Essentially having correctly laid out the demands of the law, the author goes on to explain the meaning of registration [of the church with Soviet authorities:] "Registration of church buildings and the issuance to the pastor of the documents necessary for conducting worship services is effected...only under the condition that the <u>pastor</u> and the leadership of the congregation agree <u>in full</u> to fulfill Soviet legislation concerning cults." From this correct understanding of registration, he, at the same time, draws conclusions directed toward the non-fulfillment of these laws, [with the result of] refusing registration...

III.   <u>Organizational Activity, The Direction Toward the Establishment of Children's and Youth Meetings, Circles, Groups not in Accordance [with Laws Governing] Religious Cults.</u>

Among the materials presented for expert analysis there is contained documentation testifying to the organized activity of P.V. Rumachik as it is connected to the instruction of minors and the establishment of children's and youth circles and groups...

In the "Messenger of Salvation," there is are regular columns entitled "To Parents and Children" and "The Christian Family – A Home Church," which give recommendations on conducting work for the religious upbringing of children...All of this testifies to the organization of a war against atheist upbringing as directed by the leadership of the CC-ECB in conscious violation of the corresponding established laws forbidding the organization of children's and youth meetings, circles and groups, and religious schools. Judging from the materials confiscated from him, P.V. Rumachik is an active participant in this war.

Conclusions.
...2. Judging from the materials confiscated from him, P.V. Rumachik maintains a connection with an extremist group of the CC-ECB that is conducting a systematic ideological work, the chief goal of which is the

battle for the repeal of Soviet laws concerning religion and the church...[192]

3. In the considered material there is the tendency to erect a multitude of problems that cross the boundaries of religious interests into the realm of government politics, legislation concerning cults, civil relations, scholastic education, and upbringing.

4. In the considered material there are contained the clear and direct calls to non-fulfillment of Soviet legislation concerning religious cults directed to individual Baptist congregations and the whole organization of the ECB alike in their entirety, bearing with them an anti-social character...[193]

[Submitted by:]
Grakavenko, F. I.
Expert Council, Candidate of Philosophical Sciences
November 1969

---

[192] This statement would also place the accused in violation of Article 72 of the RSFSR Criminal Codex: "Organizational activity directed toward the preparation for or the commission of especially dangerous crimes against the state, or to the creation of an organization which has as its purpose the commission of such crimes, or participation in an anti-Soviet organization, shall be punished in accordance with articles 64–71 of the present code." Articles 64–71 cover punishments for the following crimes, respectively: Treason, Espionage, Terrorist Acts (two articles), Sabotage, Wrecking, Anti-Soviet Agitation and Propaganda, and Propagandizing of war. The crimes listed in Articles 64–68 are punishable by death, effectively making membership in an Anti-Soviet organization a capital offense, depending on the opinion of the court.

[193] "Anti-social" in this case meaning "directed against society as a whole," or, "directed toward the destruction of society."